The
Alpha
Strategy

ALSO BY JOHN A. PUGSLEY
Common Sense Economics

John A. Pugsley

The
Alpha
Strategy

The Ultimate Plan of
Financial Self-Defense

Published by

Stratford Press
LOS ANGELES

Distributed by
Harper & Row
New York

This book is sold with the understanding that neither the Author nor the Publisher is engaged in rendering legal or accounting services. Questions relevant to the practice of law or accounting should be addressed to a member of those professions.

The Author and Publisher specifically disclaim any liability, loss, or risk, personal or otherwise, which is incurred as a consequence, directly or indirectly, of the use and application of any of the contents of this work.

International Standard Book Number: 0-936906-04-9

Library of Congress Catalog Card Number: 81-50893

To my wife Gloria
and my children
Joseph, Hollis, and Tamara.

alpha (al'fe), *n.* [Gr. < Heb. *aleph*] 1. the first letter of the Greek alphabet (A, a). 2. the beginning of anything.

strategy (strat'e-ji), *n.* [Fr. *strategie*; Gr. *strategia*, generalship < *strategos*, general], 1. the science of planning and directing large-scale military operations. 2. skill in managing or planning, especially by using stratagem.

Alpha Strategy (al'fe strat'e-ji), *n.* 1. the first plan for any individual to protect his wealth. 2. the best plan for protecting the basic savings of any individual during periods of monetary turmoil.

CONTENTS

PREFACE

The basic idea for *The Alpha Strategy* resulted from a study of economics in general and from many years of experience in investment markets. It would not have been possible to develop this simple concept without the foundation of rational economic theory provided by the cumulative work of a dozen major economists whose careers span the last two hundred years.

My single greatest benefactor in the area of rational thought is a great teacher who I believe would prefer to go unnamed. His innovations in the field of volitional science, and his penetrating analysis of society offered me my first glimpse of the simple, natural laws that govern human behavior. Courses at his private enterprise educational institute provided me with the most profound intellectual experiences in my life, and permanently altered my view of the world. Although most of my writing has been influenced by him, he would not necessarily agree with all my arguments, nor with my ultimate conclusions.

I credit the stream of knowledge which constitutes the "Austrian" school of economics with providing the basis of my understanding of investment values. Built on the foundations of Adam Smith's monumental book, *An Inquiry Into the Nature and Causes of the Wealth of Nations* (published in 1776), and the work of the English economist David Ricardo, the Austrian school actually started with Carl Menger in the nineteenth century. The ideas were refined and expanded by Eugen von Bohm-Bawerk, and then, in this century, the Austrian theory reached a new peak with the publication of Ludwig von Mises' *Human Action*.

I owe a particular debt of gratitude to Frederic Bastiat, the
nineteenth century Frenchman whose brilliant, common-sense
illustrations of the fallacies behind government interference in the
free market have been an inspiration to all workers in my field. His
tradition of clear thinking and simple exposition have been
admirably carried on in this country by the venerable Henry
Hazlitt, whose small book *Economics In One Lesson* has been a
powerful force in dissolving the confusion that emanates from the
mouths and pens of the majority of establishment economists.

All of these scholars and writers have influenced a modern
generation of teachers to whom I owe the most immediate debt of
gratitude. The writings and speeches of Murray Rothbard, Jay
Snelson, Robert LeFevre, Hans Sennholz, Benjamin Rogge, and
Harry Browne have formed many building blocks in my understanding of money and government, and I owe them all a large
debt. Both Burton Malkiel and David Dreman have made
important contributions to my views of the stock market. Jim
Duane contributed many ideas on investing in wine.

The development of the specific ideas for *The Alpha Strategy*,
as well as the structure of the book, was enhanced by discussions
with numerous friends and acquaintances, the most important of
whom was Winston Griepp. His careful analysis of the ideas
contained in the book not only made it a more consistent and
cohesive work, but also helped me to better understand the
economics that I purport to explain. Robert Kephart, Douglas
Casey, John Finn, Wallis Wood, and Frank Vita also contributed
valuable insights and ideas that enhanced the concept and the
finished work.

I also appreciate the help of the numerous individuals employed
by manufacturing and retailing firms around the country who
patiently supplied the data on products mentioned.

The rough manuscript was read by Dick Taylor-Radford, John
Finn, Ginger Durkee, Charlene Snodgrass, and Hollis Pugsley, all
of whom offered valuable suggestions that were incorporated into
the finished work. Carol Cardwell was my primary assistant on the

book, and was responsible for the majority of research work, as well as being an indispensable critic and editor. Estelle Doyle was the primary editor of the manuscript, and her revisions substantially increased the readability of every chapter.

I owe much to my wife, Gloria Terry, for forcing me to expunge redundant, extraneous, and overly wordy sections from the book. She made each reader's task much easier.

Obviously, the final conclusions and any errors or omissions are solely my own.

INTRODUCTION

"These are the times that try men's souls," said Thomas Paine in *Crisis,* as he described the agony being endured by Americans during the most turbulent years of the American Revolution. The lives we lead today have little in common with those led by the colonists, yet those words still seem hauntingly appropriate to our own era. For all the affluence, comfort, and convenience of life in late twentieth-century America, most individuals still face an anxious, uncertain struggle for economic security.

Will we survive financially? Will we enjoy the same food, shelter, automobiles, vacations, and other amenities of life that we have in past years? Or will the future mean less of those things, and more hardship and sacrifice as the world around us becomes more turbulent?

An average citizen in an industrialized nation today can't help but feel uncertain about the future. From every newspaper, magazine and bookstand, from every newscaster and commentator, and from every politician and philosopher come warnings of dire peril for our way of life. We are told that we are running out of natural resources, that we are destroying our environment, that we must learn to get along with less, and that we must sacrifice for the survival of the nation and the species. We wait in gasoline lines. We wince at the rising cost of hamburger and bread. We learn of layoffs in the local auto plant. We wonder whether we will be able to send our children to college, or meet a sudden medical expense, or be secure when we grow old.

The anxiety gripping us is not unfounded. There really *is* a crisis
in our lives and the future really *does* hold economic trauma. In
fact, the future is far less safe than most people imagine. Even in
his anxiety, the typical working person in America has a far more
optimistic view of the future than is warranted.

Most individuals are relying on better times ahead to take care
of problems they can't handle today. A person struggles to meet
expenses but doesn't sacrifice inordinately to save for tomorrow,
because tomorrow there will be a windfall; tomorrow there will
come a raise, or a better job, or more business, or more time.
Individuals rarely invest significant amounts of time analyzing
world economics because they assume they are too ignorant to
understand economics, and besides, perhaps tomorrow someone
in power, some brilliant leader, will stop inflation and recession.
Tomorrow the government will bring us back to prosperity. Our
job will be secure. Our savings will be secure. Life will be secure.

Belief in tomorrow's prosperity is an unfortunate and costly
illusion. It results from a lack of understanding of basic economic
laws. The financial problems constricting our lives are the
consequences of ignorance. The future depends on whether
enough people understand how they are being victimized in time to
take action to defend themselves. At this point in history, there is
no evidence to support the idea that even a small minority of
people understand the source of their problems; therefore, we must
assume that the future holds a continuation and acceleration of
past trends. If this is true, get ready for more inflation, more
frequent and deeper recessions, and a deterioration of your ability
to preserve your wealth.

The Alpha Strategy gives you two things: first, a clear understanding of how our economic system is victimizing you; and,
second, a four-level strategy for preserving your savings and
defending what's left of your personal freedom against the growing
plunder of the State. While delivering these two critical benefits,
the book also explains the world monetary system in terms you can
understand, and provides a totally new lens through which

traditional investments can be viewed and understood.

Be ready for a massive restructuring of your beliefs. Exposure to these new ideas could lead you to conclusions about the society in which you live that will be totally opposite to almost everything you have been taught in school, and to almost everything you have heard or read in the news media. When you have finished Part 1, you will have a new view of the world around you—a more realistic and valuable perspective on human society. This knowledge can arm you against the economic turmoil ahead.

A word of caution. The description of social plunder in Part 1 may seem irrelevant to your immediate problem of protecting your savings, and you might decide to skip immediately to Part 2. However, comprehension of Part 1 is the essence, the heart of the Alpha Strategy. It is essential that you understand Part 1 *before* you can implement the Strategy.

Finally, all savings and financial planning, no matter how well done, will be worthless if the present direction of society continues. The Fourth Level of action, described in the final chapter, is by far the most important aspect of the Alpha Strategy. It should be read last, carefully, and thoughtfully. Your financial survival, your physical survival, and the very survival of the species depends fully on how many people comprehend, and how carefully they act.

March 15, 1981

Part 1

The Problem

Frankly, dear public, *you are being robbed.* This may be put crudely, but at least it is clear.

—Frederic Bastiat, *Economic Sophisms*

CHAPTER ONE

THE STING

Welcome to the world's greatest carnival, the American economy. Here you can take a chance at winning the American Dream. You can work hard, save your money, invest it wisely, and win that coveted prize--financial independence. All it takes is the three virtues: hard work, thrift, and investing in America.

But wait. You say you tried it and came away disappointed? You worked hard, saved, even bought a few stocks, and all you have to show for your effort is a tiny savings account that is evaporating with inflation, a job that is threatened by recession, and a few stocks that rise and fall like roller coaster cars?

Maybe you had a run of bad luck. Perhaps, as your political leaders tell you, all this inflation is just an aberration that will go away tomorrow. Perhaps, as your stockbroker tells you, the market is really going to come out of the doldrums and go up again for another twenty years, as it did in the fifties and sixties. Perhaps the government will finally get control of the business cycle and your job will be stable and secure. Perhaps you should just keep trying.

Well, before you chalk your experience up to a run of bad luck and jump back into the pursuit of the American Dream, come along with me. You deserve a trip behind the scenes to see for yourself what is really going on. All is not what it appears to be. The rich prizes dangling before the struggling middle-class American— enticing him into working hard, voting for progress, and saving and investing with our great financial institutions—are bait. Like the prizes displayed on the boardwalk of a carnival, they attract the innocent so that they can be fleeced by the operators; behind the flashy facades of the world of money and business, there is some skullduggery going on.

The disappointments you have had in trying to work, save, and get ahead are not the results of bad luck but of an exceedingly sophisticated and brutal con game in which you are the unwitting and *almost* helpless victim. You are the target of the greatest sting in the history of mankind—a sting that makes all other con games in history look amateurish. The take is big—hundreds of billions of dollars every year—and most of it comes from hardworking, trusting, middle-class citizens just like you. To give you an idea of the magnitude of your loss, you are being steadily fleeced of about half of everything you earn and, in the long run, of the majority of everything you save.

You are going to be surprised at how the sting works. (Every sting, to be effective, must be clever enough to defy detection.) Moreover, you will be downright shocked to find out who it is that is ripping you off. The culprits are people you would least suspect—clever manipulators who have even convinced you to participate in your own demise.

The danger to your wealth today does not come from errors of judgment on your part; it comes from a group of individuals indoctrinated with the idea that your wealth should belong to them—individuals who have developed such a sophisticated system of plunder that almost no one, from the small investor with a tiny savings account to a professional investment manager with millions under his control, truly understands how the sting is taking place.

Before you can understand the sting, you must first shed all the false ideas that our educational system and the news media has taught you about economics. Economics happens to be one of the simplest, easiest, and most useful subjects a person can learn. Of course, that is not what we are told, and certainly, the way the subject is mangled and distorted in most books and articles, one would think it is obscure, difficult, and boring. Even if you haven't studied economics in school, you have been influenced by the mumbo-jumbo of economists, for their warped thinking is translated every day for you in your newspapers, magazines, and news broadcasts. In order to understand how the sting really works, let me take you through a very brief course in real, rational economics. You will be pleased to find out just how simple things really are.

The Nature of Wealth

Everyone knows what wealth is. Yes? As a matter of fact, no. Most people have only the haziest concept of the real nature of wealth, and a hazy concept usually means a complete misunderstanding. Without a clear understanding of the nature of wealth, the odds for acquiring and keeping it are slim.

Let us begin by establishing a clear, concise definition. *Tangible wealth consists of all the real products produced by man from the raw materials of nature, and by the use of which man derives survival, comfort, and pleasure.* Tangible wealth includes such things as shoes, ping-pong balls, movies, Coca-Cola, automobiles, cheese souffles, light bulbs, mousetraps, brassieres, newspapers, yachts, and houses. There is also intangible wealth. It consists of knowledge and ideas, the things we must have in order to produce tangible wealth. Here, our concern is with tangible wealth— usable, consumable things—for it is in this area of economics that we are losing the most.

Note that the above definition of tangible wealth excludes the item most people think of when they refer to wealth—*paper money*. Paper money, as it exists in the modern world at least, is not wealth. Originally, paper money was merely a warehouse receipt for commodity money—i.e., gold or silver. Today's paper money cannot be redeemed at any fixed rate for anything. It is merely a *claim* on real wealth, redeemable at a floating rate determined by each individual who is willing to accept it. You can't eat paper money, wear it, ride in it, nor do anything else with it except exchange it for real wealth. Paper money is not wealth, it is only a paper claim on wealth. Before you wave this apparently small, but crucial distinction aside, hold your mind open. Later I will prove to you that including paper money in the concept of wealth is the mistake that has led the world into the incredible monetary nightmare that makes this book necessary. When I have finished, you will never again make the mistake of defining wealth in terms of paper money.

The Source of Wealth

Once we define wealth as those things that individuals produce from the raw materials of nature, it becomes obvious that *the only source of wealth is individual effort.* You cannot eat without first growing, cleaning, and preparing the food. You cannot wear clothes that have not been made, nor get the cloth to make them without growing the cotton, spinning the thread, and weaving the fabric. You cannot get a drink of water from the faucet unless someone has mined the ore, smelted the metal, forged the faucet, constructed the pipe, and dug a well or made a dam to catch the water. For the most part, wealth is not there for the taking; it is created by human effort.

If individual effort is the source of wealth, what is the source of effort? Why are people willing to work to produce things? For one reason: individuals work in order to gain the wealth work brings. *The primary reason for work is reward.*

Imagine yourself cast ashore on a remote island, in the tradition of Daniel Defoe's Robinson Crusoe. You are hungry, so you search for food. You are thirsty, so you labor to construct a device for catching rainwater. You are cold, so you work to build a shelter from the rain and wind. All these things you are working for are forms of *wealth*. You would not labor except that you prefer to expend a little work in exchange for the pleasures that eating, drinking and shelter bring you. You work for *personal gain*.

Nor will your effort stop when you have merely satisfied your basic hunger and thirst. You will soon want more than rainwater to drink and fruits and berries to eat. You'll be dreaming of a cold beer, a soft bed, a bowl of hot soup, and some warm clothing. These things require more work, and work you will. Soon, if you're clever, you'll have a vegetable garden, some animals to raise for milk and meat, a bed made of soft leaves, moccasins, and cooking utensils—in short, you'll be on your way to the good life. Why am I certain this will happen? Because it is our biological nature to try to survive, and to do so in as much comfort as possible.

On the average, our individual desires for comfort and pleasure border on the infinite. We tire of walking, so we tame an animal to ride. We want more comfort, so we invent a carriage for the animal to pull. We want more speed, so we invent a horseless carriage. Still not satisfied, we invent self-starters, automatic transmissions, electric windows, and stereophonic music systems. Each invention adds more pleasure and more comfort, *yet it would seem that there is no point at which the individual is truly satisfied.* There is always more comfort to be gained, more time to be saved, and more new pleasure to achieve.

Apparently, each of us is trapped in an endless quest for a higher standard of living, which is to say we have an insatiable appetite to increase the amount of wealth we consume. This idea bothers many, and leads some to conclude that this desire for ever more tangible wealth is the darker side of human nature, and that it is somehow the root of our social problems. These individuals admonish us to be satisfied with what we have, or what our grandparents had. An interesting hypothesis, but irrelevant to members of the human race. Our curiosity and our desire for comfort and survival are part of a biological heritage that stretches back millions of years. We are what we are, and wishing us different is futile. We are stuck with always wanting more than we have. So how can we get more? We must produce more.

More production seems to be a common goal of people throughout the world. Whether democratic, communist, or fascist, each government claims to have as its primary goal a higher standard of living for its citizens. The only disagreement appears to be over the best method for increasing production and raising mankind's standard of living. Each theory of social organization— democracy, communism, fascism, socialism—claims to offer the answer. Unfortunately, all of these theories have flaws that lead not to more production for everyone to consume but rather to less production for everyone to fight over. As average individuals, you and I might assume that if the great academic and political minds of the world are unable to understand these problems, or to find solutions, we could never hope to do so. In fact, the problem is far simpler than you would imagine. Understanding the problem and its solution is really just a matter of common sense. Society is nothing more than a large group of single individuals. In order to understand society you must understand how a single individual thinks and acts. Since you are an individual, if you understand what motivates you, you can understand society. Let us return to the island.

Once cast onto your deserted island, all you need do to raise your standard of living is work hard and create more wealth. The more wealth you create, the higher your standard of living. As your work improves your life, you will be stimulated to work even harder. Successful effort begets more effort.

But it works the other way, too. Anything that destroys or steals away your wealth, or anything that causes you to abandon your labors and thus reduces production, will cause your standard of living to fall. If you try to grow a vegetable garden and the wild pigs keep breaking down your fence and eating your plants before you can harvest them, you will shift your labor away from growing the vegetables and devote it instead to either doing battle with the pigs, building stronger fences, or doing something else that yields greater wealth for the effort involved. The theft of your plants by the pigs could lead you to give up gardening altogether.

In the same way, if *other people* rob you of the fruits of your labor, that, too, will discourage you from continuing to work. Again, you will be forced to devote your energy to defending your property, and that will take away from the time you have to produce. Moreover, if someone is successful in stealing from you, that person will have no incentive to produce things himself, and thus his production will fall. Theft destroys your incentive to work, as well as the thief's.

The important conclusion to be derived from this is that *theft ultimately results in lower production, and thus in a lower standard of living for the average member of society*. This is the most important conclusion that you will get from this book. If you understand it—really understand it—that understanding will alter almost every economic action you take. Theft is not a moral problem; it is a practical problem. Theft destroys production, and everyone, even the thief, eventually loses.

Value

You've been cast ashore, and are struggling to meet all your needs. How do you decide whether it is better to spend your efforts weaving a net for fishing or gathering firewood to keep yourself warm? You simply give it a little thought and you decide which you would rather have. In other words, you place a *value* on fish and a value on fire, and choose the one of greater value to you. If you are cold but not too hungry, you may choose to gather wood; if you are hungry but not too cold, you may decide on the net. There is no absolute right or wrong involved, or at least none that you can perceive from your vantage point. Your choice is based on your personal judgment of the relative value of the two goods, fish versus fire. No other person in the world could have better judgment than you in this matter, for it is *your* hunger and *your* comfort that is being satisfied.

This leads to another very important conclusion. *There is no such thing as absolute value; value is relative.* There is no standard of value that is fixed by nature; every value choice is relative to the individual making the choice. The value of anything is completely subjective. Wood is not intrinsically more valuable than a fishnet, nor is gold intrinsically more valuable than water. There is only one person confronted with a choice among alternatives. There is only one person who determines whether you prefer fish rather than fire, gold rather than water, or shoes rather than gasoline. That person is you. Your decision is always correct for you, and anyone else's opinion is meaningless.

Price

This leads to the next concept, price. You may think that price is a few numbers (with a decimal point thrown in) scribbled on a small tag dangling from something you'd like to buy. That's only one example of price. Price is a measure of the rate of exchange between one thing and another. It is a measurement of the value you place on an object or activity. Even if you are alone on your island, everything you want still has a price attached. If you are willing to spend two hours gathering firewood, those hours, that effort, is the price of the wood. If you are willing to spend two days making the fishnet, two days of labor is the price of the net. Price is the rate at which you will trade something you have for something you want.

The Price-Value Link

When we trade, we are demonstrating conclusively that we *value* what we want more than we value whatever we are offering to trade. If I pay the baker fifty cents for a loaf of bread, it is not because the bread has an intrinsic, measurable value of fifty cents. It is because I have fifty cents and I value the bread more at that moment than I value the fifty cents. On the other side, the baker values the fifty cents more than he values the loaf of bread. Once I have the loaf of bread, I may not want another at the same price. The second loaf may have less value for me. It follows then, that value is relative to the *quantity* of a thing I already possess as well as to the point in *time* at which a judgment is being made.

Our wants are endless, and each time one is satisfied it disappears and another pops up to take its place. We each have a scale of values, and everything in our individual worlds arranges itself in an order of priority on that scale. Whenever we notice something we don't have is higher on our scale than something we do have, and we find someone who has the reverse situation, we make an exchange. Things are constantly rearranging themselves on our scales. Thus, values fluctuate for us as our situations change. One moment we are willing to pay one price for something, the next moment perhaps more or less. In the marketplace, the prices of goods merely reflect the average values individuals place on the goods and services produced. Looked at in this way, it should be obvious that there can be no such thing as a fair or an unfair price. Price is a result of values, and values are individual judgments.

Plunder

This is a book about plunder—plunder that robs you of the fruits of your work; that diminishes your happiness; that reduces your incentive; and that keeps you in economic bondage.

When you think of theft, you probably think of acts in which burglars, pickpockets, or thugs use simple, direct force to take what is yours. Theft also takes the form of fraud. Instead of force, the thief promises to trade you some good or service. You agree to a trade, and give him your goods, but he sneaks away before fulfilling his end of the bargain. It is fraud when someone writes you a bad check, purposely avoids paying a bill after buying something from you, or cheats you in a business transaction. In most societies, theft by force and fraud are illegal and the government is supposed to protect you from them. Unfortunately, the government is relatively ineffective in stopping them, so almost all of us have lost things directly to thieves who use illegal force or fraud.

Yet *illegal* theft is a relatively minor problem. Over your lifetime, it is doubtful that it has cost you more than a small percentage of what you have produced. As soon as you have been hit by thieves once or twice, you develop measures to defend your property: you become more cautious in your contracts to avoid being defrauded, and you put better locks and alarms on your property to foil burglars. It is not these illegal forms of theft that this book deals with. Here I am going to expose in detail another form of theft—legal theft. Let us call it plunder. Plunder is far more dangerous and far more difficult to expose and defend against than illegal theft. For every dollar stolen from you by a con man or burglar, a thousand have been taken from you, both by force and by fraud, under the guise of law. The thieves plundering you are not hiding in some back alley. You deal with them every day. You shop in their stores, buy their products, work with them and live next door to them. They are all around you. But the sting is so clever that you don't even realize you are a victim.

The wealth you lose directly to these swindlers is substantial, but it is not your only loss. As the success of these swindlers has grown, more and more producers give up the effort of production and join the plunderers. As the number of producers dwindles, production falls, and society's standard of living falls as well. You are carried along in the slide.

You are told by politicians, economists, and social scientists that man's standard of living has reached its peak, is now falling and will continue to fall, and that we must be content with less. These experts point to the evidence: world economic turmoil, the unrest of the third-world nations, and inflation and stagnation of industrialized countries. They blame the problem on overpopulation, dwindling natural resources, and the selfish nature of man. Poppycock! The "experts" have totally missed the real cause of our problems. Our standard of living will stop growing and will fall for one reason: the systems of plunder have become so incredibly large and sophisticated that the individual's desire to be productive is being destroyed. Economic crises, labor strife, inflation, and social upheaval are merely symptoms of a growing plunder. If you are a producer, you are the victim of the plunder, as well as the victim of the social turmoil. You must begin to build your defenses against plunder. The first step in self-protection is to accurately identify and expose the plunderers.

Legal plunder is that process by which one individual uses the power of government to either control your right to exchange your property, or to confiscate your property directly. It is carried out in three ways: through inflation, through taxation, and through regulation. In the following chapters, I show you the con men's schemes, how they camouflage them so thoroughly that you even assist them, and how you can defend yourself.

Summary

Now that we have touched on a few of the most basic points in human economics, let me recapitulate these truths by stating them as economic laws.

1. An individual's primary incentive to work is to increase his wealth.
2. When work is rewarded, production rises; when it is not rewarded, production falls.
3. Plunder causes the rate of production to fall.
4. When production rises, the standard of living rises; when production falls, the standard of living falls.
5. Value is not absolute; it is the subjective judgment of the individual making the choice to trade or not to trade.

From these laws we can deduce that a higher standard of living can only come from more production, and more production will only result from a system that rewards individuals in direct proportion to the amount they produce. A higher standard of living cannot result from any system that takes a person's production away from him. Further, we can deduce that one man or any group of men cannot set values for other people. Each of us is the sole judge of what is valuable to us, and each of us should have the right to set any price we want on the things we own.

These economic principles are ironclad rules of human nature that will not and cannot be changed. They are the essence of the human animal, the nature of the beast. They may appear to be obvious when stated in this simple way, but they are far from obvious to most people in society. Let us step into the real, everyday world in which we live and work and see how ignorance and attempts to deny these principles have encouraged the growth of plunder, and have led to a world filled with conflict—to inflation, depressions, strikes, terrorism, and war. Let us uncover the crafty schemes of the con men.

CHAPTER TWO

INFLATION

We will start with the most significant, the most pernicious, and the most misunderstood of all the methods of economic fraud that are being directed against you: *inflation*. To most of us, inflation means a rise in the average level of all prices for goods and services. It is not an increase in *one* price, or in *some* prices, but an increase in the average of all *prices*.

Without question, inflation is the most deadly of economic evils. It knows no geographical boundaries. It respects neither sex, nor race, nor creed, nor state of health or wealth. It has a more destructive effect on the lives of individuals than all other forms of plunder put together. It has been with mankind for thousands of years, has surfaced in every civilized society, and has been almost universally feared and denounced. To observe its constancy throughout history, one would think it is a blight of nature, like earthquakes or the common cold, that must be suffered and accepted. Everyone claims to be its enemy, yet it defies the best efforts of the most astute and educated economists and leaders to stop it.

The rate of inflation will affect your job, the value of your savings, the way you spend your money, and all your future plans.

Each year, you make thousands of decisions that are influenced, whether you know it or not, by your estimate of whether prices are going to rise or fall. If you believe that prices might fall, you will wait to purchase that new automobile until next year. You will try to save more money now, knowing it will buy more tomorrow. You may sell your stocks and buy bonds. On the other hand, if you think prices are going to rise, you may try to spend your money now instead of saving it. You may sell your bonds and buy some real estate. Or take a trip abroad while you can still afford it. A foreknowledge of next year's inflation rate would give you an immense financial advantage over others.

Most people, including even professional economists, are hopelessly inept at predicting tomorrow's price increases, since most people have no idea as to inflation's real cause. To predict it, you must first understand it.

Take the following brief test. Below are listed the seven most common things believed to contribute to a general rise in the price level. Indicate whether you think each does or does not directly contribute to inflation by putting a check in the appropriate box. Think carefully.

		YES	NO
1.	*Profiteering.* When a businessman raises the price of his product, this causes prices in general to rise.	☐	☐
2.	*Labor Unions.* When unions demand *and receive* higher wages, it forces manufacturers to raise prices. This contributes directly to inflation.	☐	☐
3.	*Monopoly.* When one company controls the output of a product, it can arbitrarily set the price higher than the price would be if there were competition. Such practice raises the general price level.	☐	☐

4. *Cartels.* When a group of producers (such   ☐   ☐
    as OPEC) controls the supply of a product
    and arbitrarily demands a higher price than
    would be set by a competitive market,
    especially when that product is used in the
    manufacture of almost all other products,
    this causes prices in general to rise.

5. *Scarcity.* When a product become scarce   ☐   ☐
    (which occurs when bad weather causes
    poor crops, or when strikes or other
    disruptions interfere with production), its
    price rises and this contributes to higher
    prices in general.

6. *Exports.* When products are exported over-   ☐   ☐
    seas (such as occurred when the Russians
    bought large amounts of American wheat
    in 1973), the resulting scarcity in domestic
    markets causes prices in general to rise.

7. *Too Much Money.* When the supply of   ☐   ☐
    money grows faster than the supply of
    goods and services in the economy, this
    causes prices in general to rise.

I assume that you probably answered yes to most of the questions. If you did, you are in agreement with most of the economists, politicians, and financial experts in the world. Unfortunately, not all of the questions should have been answered with a yes. To understand why, let's take a brief trip back to that island on which you were shipwrecked and see how inflation might have taken place there.

Imagine that you have been cast ashore and have been

struggling to provide yourself with food, shelter, and a few rudimentary comforts. One day, to your delight, you come across another castaway, a man by the name of Maynard. It turns out that Maynard is an economist. You look on this as a stroke of good fortune, for now there are two of you, and with his brains and your skills, survival should be possible until help arrives.

You have finished weaving your fishnet and find that if you work diligently you can catch two large fish a day with it. Maynard is a failure as a fisherman, but he has cultivated a small patch of wheat and has found that, with some effort, he can make and bake two loaves of bread a day. You have tried breadmaking and found that the most you could make was one loaf per day. It seems sensible to divide up the labor, letting each person do what he does best. Each day you fish and he bakes, and you trade him one of your fish for one of his loaves of bread.

The two of you have your own little economy with a gross national product (GNP) you measure as four 'units' of goods: two loaves of bread and two fish. When you exchange a fish for a loaf of bread, you have each established a *price*. The price of a fish is one loaf of bread, and the price of a loaf of bread is one fish. Keep this definition in mind: *price is nothing more than the exchange ratio between two items*.

When fishing is bad and you only catch one fish, or when something happens to interrupt Maynard's breadmaking, your GNP falls and the two of you have less than four units of goods to consume. Usually, the person who comes up with a smaller supply of his product raises the price to the other person. If you catch one fish, you trade Maynard half a fish for one loaf of bread, and vice versa. On the other hand, when fishing or breadmaking is particularly good, your GNP and standard of living rises. If you catch three fish instead of two, you tend to lower the price, offering one and one-half fish for a loaf.

There is a reason that you adjust your price up or down as your supply decreases or increases. If fishing is good but you still try to charge Maynard a whole fish for a loaf of bread, Maynard may find it more profitable to spend a portion of his day fishing. He may then find that he can catch two fish in half a day, and still bake one loaf of bread. He won't be willing to give you a loaf of bread that takes him half a day to make in exchange for one fish that he could catch in a quarter of a day. In other words, if you don't price your product approximately proportionate to the effort required to produce it, Maynard will compete with you until you are forced to bring your price into line. On the average, however, you both create two units a day, so your price tends to stay level at one loaf of bread for one fish.

One evening, as you and Maynard are relaxing by the fire, you begin reminiscing about home, and the comfortable standard of living you each enjoyed before your misfortune. Soon the conversation turns to inflation. Maynard's eyes light up. "Perhaps," he says, "we can use my training in economics to improve our situation. It is common knowledge among the more enlightened economists that a little inflation is healthy for an economy. I think that what we need is a little inflation to get things going."

You're dubious, but you concede that you would like to get higher prices for your fish, as he would for his bread. If it really is possible that inflation results when individual producers raise their prices, then it should be easy for you and Maynard to prove it, since you're both willing to do anything possible to bring it about. You both decide that inflation must be what you need, and you agree to work together to *cause* prices to rise.

Maynard proceeds to make a list, like the one in the test you took, of all the things he knows cause inflation. "The first thing that causes inflation," he says, "is when a businessman gets greedy and raises his prices. If I raise my price for bread and charge you a whole fish for only half a loaf of bread, thereby keeping a loaf and a half for myself, that should do it, right?"

"I guess so," you reply. "But isn't it true that unions also cause inflation? If I pretend that I have a fisherman's union I'm dealing with, and union members demand a greater share of the fish for their wages, I'll have less myself and so I'll have to raise my price to you. I'll have to charge you a whole loaf of bread for half a fish. That should do it, too."

"Certainly," agrees Maynard. "Now it's obvious that I have a monopoly on bread here on this island, so I control the price and can set my price wherever I like. So if I set it higher, that will certainly insure inflation. Come to think of it, there's not much difference between my having a monopoly or a cartel. Even if there were other breadmakers, as long as I could get them to set their prices as high as mine, we'd still have inflation."

By this time, you are both getting excited about the prospect of raising your prices and the higher standard of living you'll both enjoy as a result.

"One last idea," adds Maynard, "scarcity also causes inflation, so we'll have inflation automatically any time you don't catch enough fish, or my wheat crop gets wiped out by a rainstorm."

"Or you start exporting your bread to America," you laugh.

"Definitely!" he chuckles. "Let's get started."

He walks back to his hut and you go inside yours and pick up one of your two fish. You carefully cut it in half (since you are raising your price for half a fish to a whole loaf of bread), and walk back out to the fire. Maynard is standing there with, yes, half a loaf of bread in his hand!

"Wait a minute," you exclaim. "I'm raising my price because of my union, and that means you give me a whole loaf of bread for half a fish."

"Not on your life," says Maynard. "I'm a cartel, and you must give me a whole fish for half a loaf of bread."

You pause, and Maynard continues to argue for his right to go first. He has just about convinced you to give in to his demand for a whole fish, when suddenly a thought hits you. It doesn't matter which one of you raises his price first, *either way it won't cause inflation*. (Has the fallacy of the whole thing become obvious to you yet? No? Well, read on.)

Though it appears on first glance that the price level rises when you raise the price of fish, it does not. The price *level* is the average of all prices. If you get a whole loaf of bread for half a fish, the price of fish has doubled, but what has happened to the price of bread? It has fallen in half. If Maynard goes first and you pay him a whole fish for half a loaf of bread, his price has risen, but yours has fallen.

You and Maynard may both ask for a higher price, but you both cannot get it at the same time. Whether you raise your price and he pays it, or he raises his price and you pay it, *you still haven't caused inflation, for if one price goes up, the other must come down by exactly the same amount.* It does not matter why you raise the price—whether it's a union demand, your own greed, your ability to control the product, scarcity, or whatever—these are merely your *reasons* for raising it and are irrelevant to what happens once it is raised. Raising a price does not cause other prices to rise, it causes them to fall, *providing an exchange of goods is made.*

Of course, you can both ask a higher price. Maynard can ask for two fish for a loaf of bread, and you can simultaneously ask for two loaves of bread for a fish. But no trade will occur until one of you gives in. The real price level is the level at which trades actually occur, not the level at which people would like them to occur.

In a barter society, everyone cannot get higher prices at the same time. It does not matter how many people are involved in trading, or how many products are being traded. You can start with fish and bread and then add eggs, shoes, nails, shirts, and other products, ad infinitum, and the same fact will always emerge. If one product goes up in price, one or a combination of others must fall by precisely the same amount. Since a producer cannot cause other prices to rise by raising his own price, *the one place inflation cannot come from is from the producer of products.* This is not true just in your island economy, either. In the real world, producers cannot raise the general price level by increasing their prices.

To make this clear, let's transfer this situation to the real world. Say that the United States has been importing a billion barrels of oil each year and has been paying $10 per barrel. Suddenly OPEC decides to raise the price of oil and we must now pay twice as much for the same amount. If we spent $10 billion last year, and this year the oil costs $20 billion, we are left with $10 billion less to spend on other things. Having less money, we will have to rethink what the remaining money will be spent for. We cannot buy the same things as we did a year ago. Once we have given OPEC the extra $10 billion, those products that we would have bought with that money will remain on the shelves, unsold. Of course, OPEC has the $10 billion, but will probably not choose to spend it on those items we would have bought.

The reason that it appears that the price level has increased when the oil price rises is that the producers of those unsold goods do not lower their prices immediately. They sit there with the unsold goods, hoping that their customers will return. It is called a business recession. The only way the goods can be moved, however, is if one of two things happens: either they lower their prices until they reach the point that there is enough money in circulation to buy them, or they wait until $10 billion dollars is created to replace the money paid to OPEC.

The implications of this demonstration are enormous. Individuals who produce goods for trade (and this includes all manufacturers, retailers, middlemen, laborers, union members, monopolists, members of cartels, and all the other people who are producers) are absolutely and totally incapable of causing inflation, even if they want to! Whether you raise your price because of greed, because you have a monopoly, because your union demands higher wages, or because your supplies are limited—no matter what the reason—there is no possible way you can cause other prices in society to rise as well. When you raise your price, some other price, somewhere in society, must fall by an equivalent amount, or else other products will remain unsold. Of course, every producer can ask for a higher price, but asking is not receiving. The only prices that matter are those at which trades take place, not those at which people would like them to take place.

By now you must be wondering what you are missing. It is

obvious that I'm right about the fish and bread, yet we *do* have inflation, and it is very real. Inflation in modern society comes about by a clever and almost undetectable fraud. The answer is obvious once it is properly explained. To demonstrate it convincingly, so that no misguided economist can ever confuse you about it again, I will show you exactly how it occurs. The easiest way to do this is to return once more to the imaginary island where you and Maynard were producing and trading bread and fish.

If you and Maynard expand your repertoire and begin to produce other products in addition to your old staples, bread and fish, you may soon see the advantages of using one item as the medium of exchange. Assume that the two of you now produce fish, bread, eggs, potatoes, lumber, and cloth. You decide to use fish as the barter medium, and so from now on everything will always be priced in terms of fish, rather than any other commodity. A loaf of bread costs one fish, a dozen eggs the same, potatoes are two fish per pound, and lumber is a fish per board foot. Fish has become *money*. Money is simply some commodity that becomes the accepted medium of exchange.

What happens when the supply of fish (money) increases? For example, what if you start catching ten fish per day instead of two? The value of fish (money) will fall (because the more there are, the less the value), and *all other things will tend to rise in price relative to fish (money)*.

Now if you discuss the price level, you might make the mistake of saying that all prices are rising at the same time (inflation). They are not, of course—fish (money) is falling in price. Only goods other than fish (money) are rising. Include fish (money) and the price level has not changed, because it has fallen in price as much as the other products have risen.

At last, slowly, and I hope convincingly, we are closing in on the cause of inflation. The price level can change *only if measured against a money commodity, and only when that commodity is excluded from the average*. When the quantity of money increases, the average price of all other commodities will rise, and when the quantity of money decreases, the average price of all other commodities will fall. Saying all prices are rising is the same as saying the value of money is falling. It is as simple as that. There is and can be only one single cause for inflation: the quantity of money must be increased relative to the quantity of goods.

We have found the source of inflation: *an increase in money.*

You and I cannot create money. Nor does producing real goods or services create money. In fact, production increases the quantity of goods, and if the quantity of money remains constant, prices should be falling as production rises. So again we've proven that producers are not at fault. To find the cause of inflation, we need to find out where money comes from. If you and I don't make it, who does?

CHAPTER THREE

MONEY, MONEY, WHO MAKES THE MONEY

As society grows, the inconvenience of barter becomes over-whelming. Things such as automobiles and accounting services are just plain difficult to barter with, especially when all you want is a quart of milk or a pencil. Consequently, as the population and number of products increase, individuals naturally select certain commodities to use in making exchanges. These items, by popular mandate, become money.

The items that emerge as primary trading articles are not selected by the elders of the village, the chief, the Congress or the president. They emerge naturally as the most convenient items individuals can find for this purpose. The qualities that make a good medium of exchange are durability, consistency of quality, ease of identification, portability, divisibility without loss of other basic characteristics, relative stability of supply, and finally, usefulness for something other than money.

In primitive societies, people instinctively select as money those things that are available but are relatively scarce or hard to produce and which have the qualities mentioned above. In early America, the colonists had several things they used as money including salt, hides, and Indian wampum, but the most common was tobacco. (They would have used gold and silver, and did to a small extent, but those precious metals were so scarce in the colonies that they didn't lend themselves to active trading.) Tobacco kept well, was easily recognized, could be divided into various-sized lots for making purchases of different kinds, and could be carried about without too much trouble. In some primitive cultures such things as cows, wives, stones, and even tree bark have served as the medium of exchange. Obviously, most of these things are not convenient, and their use slows down trade. As societies evolve, they move more and more towards the most convenient trading commodities for exchanges, and they usually wind up with the metals.

Metals make far better commodity money than most other things because they can be stored indefinitely, divided into large or small pieces, are easily recognized, and can have their weight and purity stamped right on them. The three metals that have the best characteristics for use as money are gold, silver, and copper. Gold and silver are both relatively scarce, meaning a small amount has a high value, and thus you don't have to carry around great weights in order to make large purchases. All three are corrosion resistant, and are easily recognized and tested for purity. As groups of people gravitate toward the use of these metals they experiment with different physical forms. Initially, metals are traded in the form of dust, chips, or bars. Gradually, it is found to be most convenient to mint the metals into coins of given weights and purities. As the metals become widely used, some individuals find they can earn a living by specializing in buying and selling them; thus, the goldsmiths and money exchangers get their start.

Concurrent with the increased usage of these metals in any society comes the problem of their storage and safekeeping. Since the goldsmiths tend to have secure vaults, individuals begin to use them as depositories. A person leaving his gold or silver with the goldsmith needs a record, so the goldsmiths issue warehouse receipts.

Two natural consequences follow. First, individuals soon find it more convenient to trade receipts rather than to go to the trouble of withdrawing their gold from the goldsmith's vault in order to make a trade, since after an exchange the party receiving the gold is likely to take it right back to the goldsmith's. Second, as transactions in these receipts become more common, the goldsmiths (or banks as we have come to know them) begin to issue bearer receipts in the form of banknotes of specific denominations. Thus, John Smith can deposit ten ounces of gold with the goldsmith, and instead of getting a receipt that says John Smith has ten ounces of gold on deposit, he can get ten individual banknotes for one ounce each, redeemable by whomever holds the note ("payable to the bearer on demand").

When money is a real commodity, like metal, whoever holds it holds real wealth. To obtain this real wealth, he has only three options. He can create it through his own effort, either by mining it or trading for it; someone can give it to him; or he can steal it by force or by fraud. In the early days, as banks became more popular repositories of gold and silver, the attraction of all that real wealth in one place stimulated the efforts of the more clever thieves. The game became a question of how it could be taken without detection. The best criminal minds in history have worked on this puzzle, and the schemes that have evolved *almost* defy discovery. Of course, governments were among the first to solve the puzzle.

The Early Embezzlers

Tribal chiefs and kings discovered early in history that there were great advantages to controlling the issuance of money. They started by minting the money metals into coins, usually stamped with their own likenesses. Ostensibly, this was the king's guarantee that there was a certain amount of gold or silver in the coin. In practice, the politicians soon found a way to turn a profit from the business.

First, they profited from "seniorage", a price charged for minting the raw metals into coin form. This was a very small percentage, though, usually not much more than the actual costs involved in the minting operation. The real profits came from debasement or clipping. After years of use, individuals would begin to trust these government coins, accepting them as being of a certain weight and fineness without weighing them. Anytime the king could not raise enough taxes to finance his wars or his preferred standard of living, he would tamper with the coinage. As the coins came through the royal treasury, he would secretly file a bit of the metal off each coin and then pass the coins off again at full value, while taking the filings and minting a few new coins. The crafty monarch might also issue new coins in which the gold or silver was alloyed with cheaper metals. Some resorted to "clad" or "sandwich" coins, in which they plated cheaper metals with gold or silver to simulate the real thing. Or again, a king might simply issue new coins of smaller size, while calling them by the same name as the older, larger coins.

In all cases the supply of gold or silver in circulation remained the same, but the supply of coins increased. The king, being the first user of the new coins, gained by the amount of real goods those new coins bought. The public, however, now had fewer goods but more coins. The result was an increase in the supply of coins that eventually led to a lower value for each coin. In other words, rising prices. The king was a thief.

Of course, the kings and politicians were not the only culprits in the game of coin debasement. Coin filing and counterfeiting was a popular ripoff among the population at large; however, the politicians wanted a monopoly on this sport, and consequently tampering with the coinage by anyone but the government was deemed illegal, and the nongovernment coin debasers were swiftly pursued and harshly punished.

You may recognize some of the old kings' tricks. It has not been that long since our own politicians used the same ploys on our coins. Gold coins were devalued, then removed from circulation. The silver content of our silver coins was first reduced, then we received copper coins clad with silver, then copper clad with nickel, and then in 1979, the infamous little Susan B. Anthony dollar. It seems politicians do learn from history, but unfortunately they learn the wrong lessons.

Banking

Coin debasement by the State was just one of many forms of fraud the money dealers developed. The bankers found an even more clever device, still in use today, called "fractional-reserve banking."

Originally, a bank was simply a depository for gold and silver, and it charged a fee to the depositor for safe storage. Bankers soon learned, however, that most of the gold and silver left in their care was never removed; depositors left it in the vaults and traded the warehouse receipts instead. If someone did make a withdrawal, someone else would probably make a deposit. A banker could loan the gold out, charge interest for the loan, and put it back again without the temporary loan being noticed. It became common practice for the banks to do this, and as long as the banker did not loan out so much that his stocks were too low to meet any requests for withdrawal by depositors, no one seemed to be hurt by the practice. In fact, the banks soon stopped charging for the safe storage of their metal and began paying interest instead. You will soon come to realize, however, that the payment of interest was no great gain to the depositors, for the loss in purchasing power that accompanied the fraud far outweighed the interest earned.

The more loans the bank could make, the more interest the banker earned. The less prudent bankers tended to make high-risk loans. These same imprudent bankers also tended to lend out more gold than was really justified by the amount of deposits they held. If a depositor became suspicious that the banker might be taking too many risks with his money, he would present his deposit receipts and demand his gold back. Needless to say, if the banker had too much loaned out, and too many depositors asked to withdraw their funds at once, the banker would not have enough gold on hand to meet all the withdrawals. At that point, his bank would collapse and any depositors who got there too late would lose their funds.

This practice of lending out part of the reserves held by the bank came to be known as fractional-reserve banking, a term which indicates that banks lend out some part of their deposits and keep only the remaining fraction in reserve to meet withdrawals. In the early days of banking, the banker himself determined what fraction of his deposits he would keep in reserve to meet withdrawals. Today that fraction is usually set by the central bank or federal government of the country involved.

Although the minute details of banking may be complex, the concept is really quite simple. Today's banks are merely financial middlemen. They borrow money and they lend money. They are money brokers, and in their regular banking activities have nothing whatsoever to do anymore with the safe storage of wealth. When you deposit your money in a bank you receive an IOU from the banker. It may be in the form of a checking-account deposit receipt, a savings-account passbook, or a certificate of deposit (CD). The IOU is a contract in which the banker promises to repay your deposit at some specific time and at some specified rate of interest. He will normally promise to repay your checking account deposit anytime you request it, so all you need to do is write a check to withdraw it. When you deposit your money in a savings account, the contract normally says the banker doesn't have to return it to you for six months or longer, even though in practice he may give it to you sooner. When he borrows your money under a CD he may not be required to return your money for a year or longer.

Bankers profit by borrowing money from depositors at one interest rate, and lending it to their customers at a higher rate. They act as financial intermediaries. Hypothetically, you could bypass the bank and lend your money to a neighbor at the rate the bank would charge, thus earning a higher return, but this is not your field of expertise. You would have to know how to check the person's credit, and would need to handle all the paperwork involved. Furthermore, you would have to be willing to undergo a loss if the person didn't repay the loan. The banker provides the credit checking service, handles all the paperwork, and takes the loss if a borrower defaults. For this he gets the interest rate differential to cover costs and provide him a profit.

At first glance it would seem that bankers provide a rather routine service between lenders and borrowers, and it might be hard to imagine how they could increase the money supply, or how they could play a role in inflation or recession. In fact, they are an important and misunderstood piece of the economic puzzle.

When the banker takes your deposit, he makes an agreement with you that he does not know for certain he will be able to keep. He agrees to return your money to you whenever you demand its return in the case of a checking account, or within a period of a few months in the case of savings and CDs. He then takes your money and loans a large portion of it (all that he is not required to keep in reserve) to someone else under a loan agreement that may not require the borrower to repay the money for as long as twenty or thirty years. If the other party doesn't repay the loan before you demand your deposit back, where will the banker get the money to repay? By borrowing from you on a short-term agreement and lending to someone else on a long-term payback, he is effectively insolvent all the time.

In practice, the banker relies on the fact that there will always be new depositors putting money in, and if you demand yours back, he can pay it out of the new depositors' money. Usually this works. However, it does not change the fact that the banker borrows short-term from his depositors and lends long-term to his clients. The banker thus makes a profit by promising something he cannot deliver unless things go just right. The law says that it is illegal for you to write a check unless the money is already in your account to cover that check. When the banker borrows short and lends long, he is essentially doing exactly what he has made it illegal for *you* to do. This is a perfect example of plunder.

The public is not aware that the banker is insolvent, for the contract between the bank and its depositors does not state that if the bank makes bad loans, the depositor may lose his deposit. When you put money in the bank, you assume that the banker will be able to repay you when you decide to withdraw your funds. If you loaned your money directly to your neighbor, you would be fully aware that the safety of your money depended on your neighbor's ability to repay, and you would make your financial plans accordingly. However, when you lend your money to the banker, and he then lends it to your neighbor, the risk becomes camouflaged. It doesn't seem to you that you have, in reality, loaned the money to that neighbor, and that you stand any risk if he defaults. But you do. When a bank makes loans, it is really risking its depositors' money. The result of this camouflage is that people make assumptions about the safety of their money, and make personal and business decisions accordingly. When economic conditions change, and when a bank suddenly finds that loans are going bad, and its depositors are withdrawing funds more rapidly than they are making new deposits, the bank can quickly go bankrupt.

How Banks Create Money

Before banks were regulated by the Federal Reserve Bank, a bank could open its doors with a small amount of gold on reserve and immediately begin making loans by issuing its own banknotes. These notes would simply say that such-and-such a bank promised to redeem the note for the specified amount of gold, on demand. The notes would circulate as money, and thus the bank was expanding the money supply in the community even though the amount of gold remained constant. A community could experience a significant business boom because of the activities of its banks, a boom which would carry on until someone decided to turn in the notes for the promised gold. If demands for withdrawal exceeded the gold in the bank's vaults, the bank would go bankrupt, and the remaining notes would be worthless.

At one time in this country there were thousands of banks issuing their own banknotes, each one valued according to the public's estimate of the creditworthiness of that particular bank. There were periodicals published that did nothing but rate the banks issuing notes and list the market prices at which the public traded these notes. Each note may have proclaimed it was worth a given amount of gold, but that had no bearing on the rate of exchange at which they would be accepted by the public.

Today, individual banks are no longer permitted to issue banknotes—the Federal Reserve now has the monopoly—but they still have the ability to expand the money supply through the mechanism of fractional-reserve banking.

When you deposit $100 into your checking account, the banker credits you with that amount of money. As far as you are concerned, you own the money and make your plans accordingly. You may decide to spend it at any time, and can do so by writing a check or making a withdrawal from your savings. The moment you make the deposit the banker loans a major portion of it (about $84 under the current reserve requirements) to someone else by making a credit entry in their checking account. This new borrower then has the power to write a check on the $84. In other words, you deposit $100 in your checking account, and the banker then deposits another $84 in someone else's checking account. The money supply has been expanded. There was originally only $100 and now there is $184. It goes even further. When that $84 gets deposited in the other person's checking account, the banker then has the ability to loan $70 of that $84 to a third person, and so on down the line. By continuing to lend and relend that same original deposit over and over again, the banking system can expand an original deposit over six times.

You might argue that the moment you withdraw your money by writing a check, the process must reverse, and the money supply must contract. Not quite, because you probably write that check to someone who then deposits it in his bank, and your withdrawal is offset by an equivalent deposit in another bank. It may be in a different bank but it is within the same banking system, which makes it act as though it were the same bank.

This expansion of the money supply has the same effect that any increase in money has. It lowers the price of money in terms of real goods, which means raising the price of real goods relative to money. Remember, price is an exchange ratio. Fractional-reserve banking is the Number Two cause of money supply expansion in society today. Now let's look at the Number One cause.

The Federal Reserve System

In the nineteenth century established banks struggled under two burdens. First, they were engaged in a vicious competitive struggle with each other, and with new banks that attempted to gain a share of the market. Second, because individuals were generally distrustful of banks and would withdraw deposits the moment they suspected a bank might be issuing too many notes, banks were faced with the constant threat of bank runs.

Using the argument that the public was often defrauded by charlatans who opened new banks and then fled with depositors' funds or who failed due to lack of sound banking practices, the established banks lobbied for government regulation of the banking industry. Of course, the established banks did not want to be controlled, they just wanted the legal power to make it difficult for new banks to enter the field, and wanted to prevent the banks that did get in from engaging in competitive practices that would affect the established banks' profits.

The established banks drew up a set of suggested banking regulations which they successfully promoted in the state legislatures. Most states then passed laws regulating the formation and operation of banks, and these laws effectively prevented upstart banks from engaging in competitive practices that would infringe on the profits of the established banks.

The problem of bank runs was approached on the federal level. Just after the turn of the century, the political power of the banking industry grew to the point where bankers were able to pressure Congress into creating the Federal Reserve System (the Fed), a central bank to control all banks in the country.

The Federal Reserve System was set up by Congress as an independent, private organization made up of the banks that belonged to it. Membership was not mandatory, but conferred certain privileges upon the member banks, and consequently most banks joined. The president was given the power to appoint a Board of Governors to oversee the affairs of the banks, and that board was empowered to establish certain rules that both member and nonmember banks had to follow. The board sets the reserve requirement (the percentage of deposits each bank has to hold in reserve), lends money to member banks, and can buy and sell U.S. Treasury securities in the public market.

It is disturbing to realize how few people understand the true purpose and interests of the Fed. Even trained economists and financial analysts mistakenly assume that the published objectives (that is, protection of the public, stabilizing the economy, etc.) are the true reasons for Federal Reserve actions. Even those who imagine that the Fed is somehow a tool of a vast conspiracy of international financiers and industrialists, fail to understand that the Fed is simply a mechanism whereby self-interested people, in this case bankers, use government to protect their interests at the expense of consumers and potential competitors.

Its promoters claimed its purposes were to eliminate panics (or recessions as we call them today) by stabilizing the supply of bank credit, and to protect the public from charlatans and crooks. In reality, the purpose of the Fed was to protect the bankers from the public. If the public could be lulled into a belief that the Fed would protect them, the established banks could expand their deposits

with much greater freedom. Federal regulation of banks
(1) enlarged the ability of the established banks to expand their
deposits and loans without the danger of bank runs and (2) further
restricted competition. The result was the Roaring Twenties, and
the aftermath was the Great Depression.

The Federal Reserve (in concert with a few other federal and
state banking agencies) determines which banks are qualified to
operate, what types of products can be offered, and what rates can
be charged. Also, in its role as overseer of the nation's banks, the
Fed has ultimate control of the expansion of the U.S. money
supply. It is in this role that the Fed most affects your life, for as we
pointed out earlier, it is the expansion of the money supply that is
the root cause of rising prices.

When the Fed wants to change the supply of money, it has three
tools at its disposal:

1. It can change the banks' reserve requirements. If it raises the
amount of reserves the banks must hold against deposits, then the
banks cannot lend out as much of their depositors' money, and the
deposits are not multiplied as greatly in the system. Thus, when the
Fed raises the reserve requirement, the money supply tends to fall.
If it lowers the reserve requirement, the money supply tends to
expand.

2. It can lend money to banks in the system. This creates a direct
expansion of the banks' reserves.

3. It can buy or sell U.S. Treasury securities.

This last tool is the most important way in which the Fed affects
the money supply, and the way in which the Fed is linked to the
spending policies of the federal government. To understand where
the majority of our inflation originates, it is essential to understand
the link between federal borrowing and the Federal Reserve.

Turning Federal Debt into Money

When Congress spends more money than it raises through
taxes, it authorizes the Treasury Department to borrow from the

public by selling Treasury bills, bonds, and notes. The Treasury offers these securities for sale at public auction, and they are bid for and purchased by banks, pension funds, trusts, corporations, individuals, and even foreign interests. These are the safest IOUs around. They are guaranteed by the government.

Inasmuch as the securities are offered at auction, there is no chance they will not be purchased. The Treasury offers such a high rate of interest that people are induced to sell their other debt securities such as bonds, savings accounts, and certificates of deposit, and buy the government IOUs.

Sale of government securities thus soaks up the savings of individuals and corporations. The more government borrows, the less money there is left for other borrowers, and so other borrowers must offer higher and higher rates of interest in order to attract funds. Rising interest rates cause the costs of doing business to rise, loans are harder to get and, as a result, business activity slows down. Both businesses and consumers curtail spending, and the economy moves toward recession.

Recessions are politically unpalatable. Idled workers and distraught businessmen hound their government representatives to do something. What they want is the availability of more money. The only way the politicians can meet the demands of their constituents is to borrow more money and spend it to subsidize business, to pay unemployment benefits to the idled workers, or to issue government contracts to buy products from the distressed companies. The government takes a dollar from one person and gives it to another as a pretense of fighting the recession. In fact, it makes things worse. Additional federal borrowing further depletes the supply of available credit and amplifies the recession.

It is widely believed that the Fed is sympathetic with the problems recessions create for politicians, and lowers interest rates in order to keep those politicians in favor with the public. That is not the case at all. The Fed is relatively insulated from political pressure and has other reasons to act. A recession means bad times for the banks. People stop borrowing, corporations lose

business, and bank profits drop. When borrowers get into trouble,
banks get into trouble. If the recession turns into a full-scale
depression, widespread bank failures may result, as they did in the
1930s. Since the Fed is an organization made up of banks, it is
clearly in the best interests of those running it to ward off the
recession by expanding the money supply.

When the Fed determines that interest rates should be lowered,
or at least prevented from rising any further, it contacts private
dealers who buy and sell U.S. government securities, and offers to
purchase Treasury bills and bonds. (Remember, these are the
same T-bills and bonds that created the rising interest rates in the
first place by absorbing the savings of individuals and corporations.) The Fed purchases these government securities and pays
for them with a check. That check is given to the private dealer, and
he deposits it in his bank. The bond dealer's bank forwards the
check to the Fed (where it has its own reserves on deposit), and the
Fed then credits the reserve account of that bank. Now the bank
has new reserves against which it can make loans. These fresh
reserves are just like a new deposit by a customer, and can be
expanded by the same process that all bank deposits are expanded.
Under reserve requirements in effect in early 1980, these reserves
can be expanded by approximately six to one; thus, when the
Federal Reserve buys $1 billion in U.S. Treasury securities, the
banks can loan out up to $6 billion to borrowers.

Where did the Fed get the money to buy the Treasury
securities? It created the money out of thin air. It credits the
reserve account of the bank by a simple bookkeeping entry. What
does the Fed have to back up its IOUs? It has the IOU of the U.S.
Treasury, that is, the Treasury bills and bonds. The Federal
Reserve accounts thus balance: they show a liability of the bank
reserves and an offsetting asset of Treasury securities. The
Federal Reserve Notes in your pocket or checking account mean
that the Fed owes you money, and these are in turn backed up by
the T-bills they hold that mean the government owes the Fed
money. The U.S. government continues to issue more and more

IOUs to cover its ever-growing deficits, and the Fed continues to buy these up and issue its own notes in their place.

This whole process is known as *monetizing the debt*. This means the debt of the federal government is turned into money. The government borrows money to meet its deficits, and the IOUs it issues eventually are converted into Federal Reserve Notes in your pocket. Those greenbacks in your wallet that you think of as money are only government IOUs broken up and reissued by the Fed.

Give it a little thought and you should see that there is no difference in the long run between the government fighting a recession by borrowing money from Peter and giving it to Paul, and the Fed fighting the recession by buying up Treasury bills and giving the banks new reserves. The only difference is a time difference. The effects of government borrowing are almost instantly offset by the effects of government spending. But when the Fed monetizes the government debt, it takes a year or more for people to offset the influx of new money by raising their prices. The Fed action just postpones the inevitable a bit longer than the government action does.

Federal deficits, then, are the root cause of continued inflation of the money supply. Once the banks have loaned out depositors' money to the maximum limit set by reserve requirements, the only source of new dollars is the Federal Reserve. The Federal Reserve, therefore, is the real engine of inflation. Its need to inflate, however, is a consequence of federal deficits.

The Future of Inflation

Now that we have identified the mechanism by which deficits are turned into money and that money multiplied, we are in a position to peer into the future and forecast the trend of prices. If we determine that the federal budget is being brought under control and deficit spending will end, we can be confident price inflation will end. If, however, we look ahead and find more or greater deficits in the future, then we must conclude inflation will continue. An estimate of future deficits should give us some indication of the inflation problem we face in the future.

Figure 1 is a graph showing the history of federal deficits in this country during the last thirty years. It is widely believed that deficits show an upward trend during wars, and usually a downward trend afterward. The upward trend during the 1960s might have been explained by the war in Vietnam, but the trend failed to change course after the war. In fact, the graph shows the opposite. During the first five years of the 1960s, deficits totalled $21 billion. During the last half of the 1960s they almost doubled, totalling $36 billion. In the first five years of the 1970s they almost doubled again, to $70 billion, and then in the last five years, ending in September of 1979, they totalled a staggering $310 billion— more than double the total of the prior *fifteen years.*

Why are deficits rising at such a frightening pace? Because the government is spending an increasing amount of money each year. The government is growing in size, and its role in the private economy is growing. This growth, however, is not the result of evil designs of power-mad politicians and bureaucrats. It is the result of an explosion in the demands made by individuals. People make the demands; politicians meet the demands.

Each year brings an increasing belief that there is such a thing as a free lunch. The government is perceived as a source of wealth. More and more people wait in line at the Treasury. The automaker requests a subsidy, the student asks for an interest-free loan, the farmer asks for price supports, the conservationist asks for a wilderness area, the ecologist for a program to stop pollution, the general for a larger defense force, the oil company for diplomatic intervention in a foreign country, the poor for foodstamps, and the handicapped for job training. Just as tiny grains of sand pile up one at a time to form a desert, so the individual requests of millions and millions of people gradually pile up, layer upon layer, until a monstrous, uncontrollable bureaucracy is created to meet their individual requests. Demands grow so large that soon they exceed

Figure 1

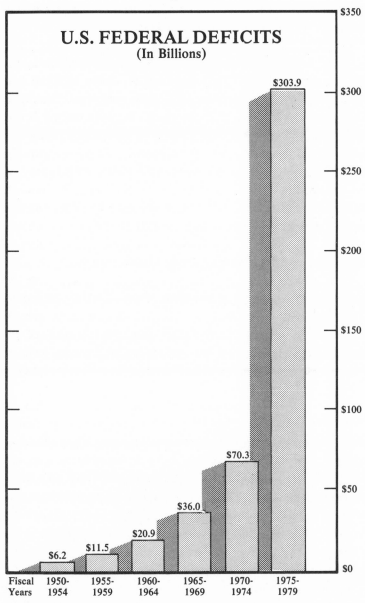

U.S. FEDERAL DEFICITS
(In Billions)

the willingness of taxpayers to support them. Rather than cut back on benefits, politicians turn to deficit spending.

It would seem that the public could be educated to recognize that government has no wealth, and anything it provides to one individual, it must first confiscate from some other individual. If the majority of individuals understood this, and further understood what disastrous long-term consequences emanate from the theft of an individual's property, then enough of them might voluntarily stop making demands on government to cause a reversal in the trend of government growth. Eventually, this would eliminate deficits and prices would stabilize. Although this is a goal to be worked for, such a change will require some method of education totally different from what has been used in the past.

There is absolutely no evidence to suggest that this type of understanding is growing either in the United States or in any other country in the world. The evidence indicates just the opposite: more and more people everywhere, every year, are becoming convinced that government should provide solutions to their problems. Consequently, every year government gets bigger and bigger, and the deficits continue to expand. On this basis alone, we must project increasing inflation in our future.

The Hidden Deficits

It would appear that demands for government spending will make it hard, if not impossible, for any politician to eliminate deficits (and thus inflation). Public ignorance is not the only thing between a balanced budget and deficits, however. There is another factor that guarantees incredibly larger deficits ahead. The growth in deficits over the past few years has been accelerating, as the chart indicates. What is not revealed, however, is a critical factor causing this sudden acceleration.

The government has chosen to report its expenditures in a way that totally camouflages the true extent of the deficit problem. To understand what they are doing, it is necessary to understand something about accounting and since most of us know little about this subject, the bureaucrats have been fairly safe with their secret. So that you may be fully aware of the problem facing you, let me expose their little subterfuge.

In accounting, there are two methods of reporting gains and losses. One is the cash method, and the other is the accrual method. If you want to find out how you fared financially during the last year, you may use either method.

To use the cash method, you simply add up all the income you received during the period, and subtract from it the total of all the bills you paid. This is the way you keep your checkbook every month. You record deposits, and subtract the checks written, and the difference is your balance. If you write more checks than you cover with deposits, you have an overdraft (a deficit). The government uses the cash method to keep its books and to report its surpluses and deficits. When the government reports a $25 billion deficit, all you know is that $25 billion more was paid out than was received.

Large businesses rarely use the cash method of accounting, preferring the accrual method instead. Why? The businessman cannot afford to kid himself. He must realistically assess his profits and losses in order to stay in business, and so he uses the most accurate method for doing so. Under the accrual method, actual cash income and cash expenses are not used to determine profits and losses for the year. Instead, the business totals up all the income promised to it that year under the terms of its contracts, and for which it has delivered merchandise, and counts this as income. Obviously, this income figure might differ from cash actually received by the firm if some customers received merchandise but delayed payment past the end of the year. On the expense side, the company shows as outgo any money it contracts to pay for goods it receives and consumes that year, regardless of whether the bill has been paid that year or not. Thus, if the company buys something but does not have to pay for it until some future year, the item is still shown as an expense in the current year.

This method of accounting makes sense for any businessman who really wants to know whether he is operating at a profit or loss. If a baker bakes 10,000 loaves of bread in a year and sells them at $1 per loaf, and receives the money in that year, he will show $10,000 of income. If he buys the flour to make that bread on credit, and does not have to pay for it until next year, his books will not show a check written for the flour. If he uses the cash method, he will show income of $10,000, but no offsetting expense for the materials used to produce that income. His profit picture is thus distorted because he has failed to take into account the real expense of earning that $10,000. Instead, the wise baker uses the accrual basis, and shows the flour as an expense, even though he will not pay for it until next year. In this way, his profit for the year is realistically shown, and he can better plan for the future.

Since the federal government uses cash-basis accounting, anything it consumes in one fiscal year but does not have to pay for until some future fiscal year does not show up as an expense. Arthur Andersen & Company, a major national accounting firm, called attention to this subterfuge in 1975 in a lengthy report titled *Sound Financial Reporting in the Public Sector*. Their auditors painstakingly reviewed the U.S. federal budgets for fiscal years ending June 30, 1973, and June 30, 1974, and came up with some shocking figures. Using the cash basis of accounting, the government reported federal deficits of $14.3 billion for 1973 and $3.5 billion for 1974. Arthur Andersen & Company recalculated the budget deficits according to the accrual method, and found that the 1973 deficit jumped from $14.3 billion to a staggering *$86.6 billion*, a jump of over $70 billion! The 1974 budget was even worse. The deficit jumped from $3.5 billion to just over *$95 billion*, an increase of over $90 billion! Thus, in just two years, the government had underreported its deficits by more than $160 billion.

Based on this Arthur Andersen report, the Treasury, under William Simon, began publishing a Consolidated Financial Statement that included accrual liabilities. These Treasury statements show Social Security debts alone (not counting veterans benefits, military pensions, or government employee pensions) of $121 billion in fiscal 1976, and $177 billion in fiscal 1977. Although these statements are published two years after the fact, conservative extrapolation suggests that the fiscal 1981 accrual deficit will exceed $250 billion. Add to this the cash basis deficit, and the true 1981 deficit winds up near $350 billion!

This is grim news for you and everyone else. No matter how sincere a political candidate appears when he promises a balanced budget in the future, he will be powerless to bring it about. A true balanced budget would require a $350 billion dollar budget cut! It is a political impossibility. Expect the largest budget deficits in the history of the nation during the next five years.

Summary

An increase in the money supply is the only cause of inflation in the long run. Money is created by banks through fractional-reserve banking, and by the Federal Reserve as it monetizes federal deficits. The future rate of inflation is primarily a function of the size of deficits, since the Federal Reserve is duty-bound to monetize them.

The message should be clear. Past debts and future demands of the public are going to drive the federal deficits beyond comprehension. The Federal Reserve will be completely helpless to resist a massive expansion of bank reserves in order to avert a banking system collapse. The money supply is going to soar, and with it will come inflation rates that will make the 1970s seem like a period of price stability. By 1985, prices will have doubled from their 1980 levels. By the end of the decade, prices may be ten times their current levels. Hyperinflation could happen here.

CHAPTER FOUR

THE EFFECTS OF INFLATION

To fully understand how the entire process of deficit spending and inflation affects your life, it is necessary to separate and examine the actions of the government and the actions of the Fed. As we do this, keep in mind two fundamental economic realities. First, resources are limited. Only a given quantity of goods is available at any moment. If a person spends his time doing one thing, it means he cannot be doing something else. If he spends a dollar on one item, it cannot be spent on something else. Second, individuals resist changing their occupations and businesses. They resist because change means an immediate sacrifice. To learn a skill or create a business requires an investment of time, energy, and money—in other words, capital. To change from one trade to another—for example, to change from being an engineer to being a psychologist—means that the individual must learn new skills, spend time in study and training, and then invest time in practicing. To change businesses means abandoning capital invested in old tools, facilities, and inventory. Starting over is costly.

The Misallocation of Capital

Resources are limited and change is costly. These facts go a long way toward explaining why the growth of government is destructive as well as so hard to contain.

When you create a product and exchange it for money, you assume control of how that money will be spent. You will spend it according to your values, trading it for the things you value the most at that moment. If you earn $100 by baking bread and choose to spend it on a suit, the tailor will benefit. He will make a profit and that profit will encourage him to invest more capital in training and equipment to enable him to make more suits. Your spending encourages capital investment in the production of things you value.

Suppose the government hits you with a $100 tax. They now have your money, and you can no longer buy the suit. The government chooses to spend the money on a sign for the subway system in Washington, D.C. Now, the businessman who makes those signs for the government is encouraged to expand his capital investment, just as the tailor would have. The government has reallocated capital. Instead of your money encouraging the production of goods you value most, it now encourages the production of goods that some bureaucrat in Washington values most.

Not only does government spending cause capital to be reallocated away from consumer demands, it also encourages waste by not rewarding the most efficient producers. You work hard for your money and, therefore, are careful to shop for full value. You try to pick a tailor who will give you the best buy for your money. The bureaucrat, on the other hand, does not work at all for the money. He spends someone else's money, someone he does not even know. Getting the most value from the money he has taken from you cannot be as important to him as getting value for the money would have been to you.

While production is encouraged by government expenditure, it is not necessarily the efficient producer who gains. More importance is placed on giving contracts to companies that offer some political benefit to the bureaucrat than to those companies offering the best products for the lowest price. Government spending is naturally wasteful.

The government reallocates capital, and does so inefficiently, but a further problem occurs when any attempt is made to slow government spending. If the government were suddenly to disappear, all those individuals and businesses dependent on government support suddenly would have to satisfy consumers in the open market. They would have to abandon much of the capital investment they had in their current products and invest time and energy to gear up for making the products demanded by consumers. Nor would consumers be willing to pamper them or subsidize them. Those producers who successfully sold products to an uncritical government bureaucrat would find a cold reception among consumers unless they could compete with businesses already meeting consumer demands. The transition would be painful for all these individuals and companies, and fatal to many. This same effect happens in a small way whenever the government cuts back on any of its programs. Cutbacks in any area are always met with cries of anguish and vigorous political lobbying from those affected.

In summary, when the government spends your money rather than letting you spend it, it misallocates productive resources, causing human energy and capital to be directed toward the production of goods that are not the choices of consumers. Once it begins doing this, change is difficult because of the reluctance of individuals to abandon previous investments. The result is a continuing growth of the bureaucracy, and an increasing misallocation of resources. Unfortunately, the problems of government spending do not stop here.

The Business Cycle

When the people who run the Fed decide to expand the money supply, an order goes out to buy T-bills. At that instant the demand for T-bills has risen, and this affects the entire market for debt securities. It means that new buying power is making a demand on the bond market, and prices for bonds will begin to rise. Interest rates are inversely related to bond prices. When bond prices rise, interest rates begin to fall. Another way to see this is to view the interest rate as the price of lendable funds. A greater supply of lendable funds means a lower price for those funds. The marketplace gets a signal that interest rates are softening.

Those investors who watch the stock market will notice this trend and will assume that it's a good time to buy stocks, since business profits tend to improve during periods of falling interest rates. Investors will also find that money for stock purchases is more available, just as businessmen will find that it is easier to borrow money. The new money issued by the Fed is at work, percolating down from the securities dealer, who received it first, to the banking system that is eager to expand its deposits and loans. Interest rates fall, bond prices and stock prices rise, and business activity picks up. The fresh money eventually reaches down to the consumer, who can now feel the effects as unemployment rates fall and consumer loans become easier to get. We are told that the economy is entering a period of prosperity.

It will not be long, however, before the new money added to the system begins to create a pressure for individuals to raise their prices. This pressure is not immediate, but may begin to be felt anywhere from one to three years after the Fed's initial purchase of securities. One after another, prices are raised to meet increasing costs, and soon the price level has ratcheted a notch higher. The increase in the money supply has been offset by an overall increase in the price level, and the economy is now in trouble. Firms that geared up to produce more goods during the boom now find themselves without customers, and soon a recession appears.

To visualize this, assume you are manufacturing shirts. Pretend your customers have a total of $100 a day to spend on shirts, and your shirts sell for $10 each. You thus sell ten shirts per day. Suddenly the government hands your customers an extra $100 per day and directs them to spend it on shirts. Faced with orders for twenty shirts per day, you scurry to equip yourself to meet the demand. You buy new sewing machines and hire new seamstresses. Things go well for a few weeks, but when you order more cloth, you find the cost has risen. Next your workers complain that they cannot get along on the wages you are paying and demand a raise. You reluctantly inform your customers that you must raise the price of your shirts to $20. Since they have a total of $200 per day to spend, they now cut their orders back to ten shirts per day. You are back where you started. Only now you have too many machines and too many workers. Your only choice is to cut back production, lay off the workers you hired, and sell your surplus machines at a discount.

Thus, expanding the money supply causes a temporary business boom. Soon the money causes higher prices. At the new higher prices, there is no longer enough purchasing power around to buy all of the products that the businessmen geared up to produce when they were first hit by the fresh money, and they are faced with cutting back to the old levels of production. This means layoffs, cancellation of orders for raw materials, and curtailment of production. The cycle has been completed, and the country faces recession once more.

There is one more distortion to add to the picture. When the Fed created the new money, that money acted as a demand on certain products. The money first makes a demand on bonds, then stocks, then production goods, and then consumer goods, in that order. The money creates a chain of false prosperity that wends its way down to the consumer. Each person who receives the money thinks himself richer, and shifts his value scale around a bit. He decides he can afford some additional goods that had formerly been out of reach—some luxury item, for example. New money tends to create a demand for luxury goods. Since we know that the investment of capital in production of one thing means that capital is withdrawn from investment in something else (since resources are limited), expansion of the luxury industries must come at the expense of other industries. Once prices rise, and a recession sets in again, those industries producing these luxuries usually find their sales falling. If their sales continue, the money they receive is drawn away from the producers of nonluxury goods, and those producers are hurt.

The expansion of the money supply by the Fed causes a chain reaction: first, a business boom, then rising prices, and finally recession. Simultaneously, the capital structure of the nation is distorted. During the cycle's initial stages, capital is allocated to the production of goods that consumers would not have purchased without the additional money. During the later stages, industries must change back again, and the adjustment hurts everyone.

A Climate for Plunder

Earlier, I said that rising prices are the reality of the future. Now I think you can see why prices themselves are not your only concern. The business cycle discussed above is far more destructive to your well-being than rising prices alone. Nor is it just the lower production—which results from the difficulties businessmen have in meeting fluctuating demand—that saps your standard of living. Business turmoil feeds back into the political arena as people become increasingly frustrated by the vacillating economy. Where do they turn? They demand that politicians do something. But the only thing politicians can do is to interfere even more in the economy. Individuals cry for immediate relief from the symptoms of inflation—rising prices, recessions, unemployment—and politicians respond with more government spending and a series of economic restrictions on business. Rising prices are met by price controls. Rising wages by wage controls. Business losses by subsidies. And then there are the antitrust laws, the labor laws, tariffs, export controls, and on and on.

Why do these laws follow so quickly? Because economic turmoil creates rich opportunities for some individuals to tap government power and use it to profit at your expense. Recession and inflation create a perfect climate for the sting, and out of the woodwork come hordes of con men and swindlers. Let us see just how they use your economic travail to pick your pocket.

Price Controls

Everyone resents rising prices. When prices rise rapidly, individuals support politicians who will take action to stop the rise. Since most people believe the person raising the price is responsible, the most obvious political action to be taken is to pass laws fixing prices or limiting profits. Price controls are not bureaucratic solutions, they are a political demand made by voters. Mandatory, across-the-board price controls have been instituted thousands of times in the history of nations (three times right here in the United States in the last forty years), and voluntary guidelines have been even more frequent. Not once in their three thousand-year history have controls or guidelines had any real effect on rising prices. The only excuse offered for this dismal history of failure has been that the controls were not strong enough or were improperly administered.

Even those who are adamantly opposed to controls ("free-enterprise" businessmen, for example) defend this philosophical position on the basis that controls fail because they are too hard to administer. In other words, they really believe that controls *could* work if an effective way could be found to force producers to comply.

Only a tiny handful of economists, mostly unnoticed, have used the correct argument against controls: they cannot possibly work, no matter how they are administered, because the individual prices at which people sell their products have nothing to do with inflation.

Since people believe producers—manufacturers, retailers, laborers, and middlemen—are responsible for inflation, price controls will be tried over and over again, and each time the public will demand that politicians develop more efficient methods of enforcing them. Since it is unlikely that the public can be educated to the fact that such controls cannot work under any circumstances, the future is clear: we will have price controls over and over again whenever we have inflation.

Price controls will not stop inflation. Instead, they reduce production. Remember Economic Law 2: When work is not rewarded, production falls. If the profit is removed, the reason for making the effort vanishes. Price controls remove profit and drive the producer out of work. Forced to quit producing the price-controlled product, the individual is driven into some other line of work for which he is not as well qualified; this results in less production.

Price controls always result in shortages of controlled products. When controls limited prices during World War II, the Korean War, and during the Nixon administration, shortages were widespread. The gasoline and heating oil shortages of recent years are further examples. A complex network of controls made it unprofitable for the producers to expand production to meet demand and scarcity was the result. Price controls on apartments (rent controls) have a clear history of creating apartment shortages wherever they have been used.

Products that are price controlled disappear from the shelves and show up on the black market where they are priced even higher than they were on the free market, because now the producer must earn an additional premium over and above his profit to compensate him for the risk he is taking in breaking the law. When everything is price controlled, so that there is no line of work into which you can switch to make a profit, then everything is in short supply (except on the black market). One needs only to look at Russia or China where all prices are dictated by the State to see this truth dramatically demonstrated.

You lose in another way to controls. The wider the controls, the greater the army of enforcers required. All the administrators and enforcers of price controls are lured away from productive jobs in private industry where they have been creating real goods and services. Their production is lost to you and to society. Remember Economic Law 4: When production falls, your standard of living falls. In addition to the lost production, you are taxed to pay the salaries of these nonproductive enforcers, and your standard of living ratchets down another notch.

Before you rush to write to your congressman about controls, however, remember that he is not the force behind them. Price controls are a prime example of the sting. They exist because A wants to buy the product of B at a price lower than B wants to sell it. Since A cannot personally force B to sell at that price, he turns to the politicians and asks for government force. The politician who votes for controls is merely serving the interests of a multitude of his constituents, all of whom are hoping to benefit from swindling other producers out of their production. If you are selling a product, whether it is your labor to an employer, your professional expertise to a client, or manufactured goods to any buyer, and your price is controlled by the bureaucracy, you lose. And in the end, the person demanding the control loses as well, for eventually the product is driven from the market and there is nothing for him to buy at all.

Wage Controls

Wages are prices. They are the price an individual charges for his time and effort. Businessmen and consumers are quick to demand that politicians do something about the outrageous wage demands made by unions, and the political answer is the sister of price controls: wage controls.

The result of wage control is just as bad as the result of price control. The controlled worker is unable to offer his labor at the price he feels it is worth because the employer has succeeded in getting the politician to force the laborer to sell it for less. The result is not less inflation, of course, because inflation is not caused by the wage demands of labor. The result is lower production. When wages are frozen while living expenses continue to rise, the worker will go on strike, will change jobs in order to get into some line of work that pays a higher wage, or will simply slow down in anger over his belief that he is being cheated. In any case, production falls. Wage controls have absolutely no effect on the inflation rate, and are destructive to production.

Wage controls are as much a part of the sting as are price controls. The person demanding controls (usually the employer) hopes to benefit at the expense of the worker by forcing him to sell his labor at a lower rate. In many cases, the employer feels justified in this use of force, since his workers may have already used government power to extract higher wages through coercive labor legislation. Even if the worker has used force, however, the employer's answer should not be more force. This tit-for-tat approach only succeeds in expanding government and lowering production even further.

Antitrust Laws

It is hard for anyone who has listened to the blistering attack on the Organization of Petroleum Exporting Countries over the past years to accept the fact that cartels and monopolies cannot cause inflation. They *cannot*. All a cartel or monopoly can do is raise the price of one product. As I demonstrated earlier, if a member of a cartel receives a higher price, some other prices must fall. People do not realize this, however, and their ignorance has opened the door for an army of swindlers. Public demands for political action against cartels, monopolies, and other "combinations in restraint of trade" translate into antitrust legislation, another prime example of the sting.

In brief, antitrust law is based on the premise that if a seller is able to dominate and control the market for his product, he can charge a higher price than he could if the market were competitive, and thus cheat the public. The laws state a seller cannot use price discrimination favoring one buyer over another, preclude a buyer from doing business with a competitor, nor acquire ownership of another company if this tends to create a monopoly.

The first fallacy can be found in the initial premise itself: that sellers can control and dominate the market. Every producer is trying to maximize his profit in the marketplace, and will raise his price as high as competition will allow. Hordes of entrepreneurs roam the marketplace searching for the highest profit opportunities to employ their skills and capital. Nor is there any lack of capital keeping them out of products requiring large investments. There are literally billions of dollars of capital available to enter any market where the profit opportunities are larger than normal. If a manufacturer succeeds in capturing the major share of a market, he must do it through sharp competitive selling. The moment he has monopolized the market and attempts to raise his prices to benefit from his monopoly, he will find a flood of entrepreneurs rushing in to compete with him and to share in the higher profit margins he is reaping. As each competitor struggles to widen his share of the market, prices will be driven down once more. This time, however, they will fall even lower than they were originally, because now there are more producers competing for the available customers.

The idea that a group of producers can band together and create higher than average prices for any length of time is also false. They may try, and may even join in a cartel agreement, but their success will be only temporary. Each member will always be looking out for himself, and will use every chance to gain an edge over the other members. Business history is strewn with the carcasses of cartel agreements that were destroyed by the competitive wrestling of the members themselves.

Those who point to OPEC as an example of an effective cartel fail to understand the facts. First, OPEC is engaged in a constant internal struggle as each member country tries to force the cartel to set price and production at levels most beneficial to itself. Second, quadrupling the price of oil in one giant step was successful only because oil had been enormously underpriced in world markets. The price had not been adjusting over the years either to inflation in the industrial countries nor to the explosive rise in demand for oil. Furthermore, the supply of oil from U.S. fields had been curtailed because of price controls and other government regulation of domestic production. Once these restrictions are lifted, production will leap in the United States, and the increased supply will automatically bring the world price into line with the price increases of other products, OPEC or no OPEC.

The second fallacy on which antitrust law is founded is that a person is cheated if someone charges too high a price for a product. This implies that one individual somehow has the right to the production of another individual. If you buy some wood and build a chair, who does that chair belong to? Does it belong to you, or does it belong to someone else? Now, if you tell me that it belongs to you, then you should be able to do with it as you please. You should be able to keep it, or sell it for whatever price you choose. If you feel that you would rather have the chair than $10, why should you be forced to sell it for $10? If you feel that the chair is worth $10,000 to you, how can someone else justify forcing you to take even $1 less?

The person who wants your chair has no real claim to it unless he can induce you to part with the chair voluntarily. The chair is a result of your effort. A person who uses government to force you to give him the chair for anything less than you would willingly sell it for is simply using force to plunder your property on the basis that his need is a rightful claim on your effort. It is clearly a case in which he feels that you should be his slave. The laws of economics clearly explain why any type of theft results in lower production and a lower standard of living for all.

To achieve a higher standard of living in a society, we must recognize the right of any individual to set any price he wants on the goods that he produces. Antitrust law is wrong, because it is based on the false idea that if you set your price too high, you are cheating your customer.

The antitrust laws are not only unnecessary, they have a profoundly destructive effect on the output of goods and services in the country. First, they are horrendously expensive to enforce. The court cases involving antitrust actions are the most expensive in the judicial system. Companies are required to supply records to the court that cost millions of dollars to compile, consist literally of tons of paperwork, and consume hundreds of thousands of hours of legal time by Justice Department attorneys. The millions of dollars of taxpayers' money used to prosecute these companies and the additional millions of dollars spent by companies to defend themselves is paid by you and me. We have less to consume because all that human effort is wasted.

The second way the antitrust laws reduce your standard of living is by preventing the most efficient producers from developing their markets in the most effective way. Where companies could lower prices by merging and more efficiently catering to particular markets, the law says they cannot do it. These laws do not accomplish their stated objectives; that is, they do not lower prices by breaking up monopolies. They force you to pay much higher prices because they prevent companies from merging and using competitive business techniques to get your business. The laws make nonsense of the very thing they are trying to accomplish. They do not promote competition; they restrict it.

Antitrust laws are more than simply a faulty concept; they are a fraud used by crafty businessmen to tap your pocketbook. They are no different than most other government regulations, in that they limit competition and thus control where you spend your money. Nowhere is the use of government as a sword of theft as easily documented as is the case of these laws. Read any of the cases of antitrust actions brought against businesses and you will almost always find the actions were initiated not by the government but by other businesses. Time and time again, you read that

Company A has filed suit against Company B for violations of the antitrust laws. Any company finding its market position threatened by the sharp marketing practices of a competitor has the opportunity to ferret out violations of these statutes and can file complaints with the Federal Trade Commission, or file civil actions on its own.

Nor is it hard to find violations. A company that sells at a price below competition is automatically suspect of discriminatory price-cutting tactics, something illegal under the laws, and something that can give the higher-priced competitor a lever for legal action. Frequently, a business buying products from another industry will find the prices, because of competition, are all nearly the same from the various suppliers. This gives the buyer the opportunity to levy charges of price-fixing, and again bring the government down on the suspected companies. The buyer also has the ability to file charges of price gouging in the event a company is charging prices higher than the competition.

In the world of antitrust, it is one businessman against another, each determined to use the sharp sword of the law as a weapon against his competitor. When the sword cuts, it always wounds or kills the business it's aimed at, and it always takes a little slice out of you, too. The businessman who can't attract your patronage through competitive pricing, quality, or service can get the government to destroy his rival and get your business by default. It is your wealth that is the ultimate target in the great antitrust sting.

Subsidy

Hardly a day passes in any modern industrial country that the news media does not carry stories about the failure of businesses. In our era of inflation-spawned business cycles, when boom and recession follow each other in metronomic procession, no business seems totally secure from bankruptcy. Businesses fail because individuals like you and I survey their products and turn down their offers. Their prices may be too high, their workmanship poor, their products outmoded, or, more likely, they have been whipsawed into trouble by inflation. In any case, competition has defeated them in the marketplace. We judge their products, count our scarce cash, and decide to spend our money on something else.

When a product is rejected in the marketplace, however, that does not always mean that the seller goes down to defeat. If we refuse to buy his products voluntarily, he still has the possibility of using force to get us to buy them. With some effort he may be able to get the government to take the money from you through taxation or borrowing to give it to him. Here is how it is done:

You sell automobiles (or airline seats, or shoes, or potatoes), and suddenly markets change. Your sales decline, your costs soar, your competition has a new ad campaign, foreign imports undercut your price, or your union strikes. You are faced with bankruptcy. You think through the ramifications of the failure of your business, and recognize that more is at stake than just your own profits. Hundreds, perhaps thousands of shareholders will lose if you go under. Banks hold millions in notes that will be worthless if you collapse. You have employees, thousands of them, who will be out of work. The businesses that supply you with parts and raw materials will have to lay off their employees. All the merchants who depend on your employees' business will be hit by recession. The ripples from your bankruptcy will spread until they touch every corner of the nation.

You have a bright idea. Why not appeal to the government for a subsidy? After all, it is in the best interest of thousands of people, perhaps the nation, to see that you do not go bankrupt. By pleading for the government to protect these others, you may be saved.

You, the leaders of your union, and the bankers who hold your notes, all converge on Washington to argue your case before the bureaucrats and politicians. The government is a stern, concerned patriarch who admonishes you, and talks about free enterprise and the rigors of competition. Its accountants pore over your books; its committees listen with caution to your tale of woe. Finally, it agrees. The nation will be better off if you stay afloat. Congress offers loan guarantees, tax reductions, and outright grants to keep your workers on the line, and your creditors from foreclosing.

A familiar story? Of course. Remember Lockheed? Penn Central? Chrysler? All have faced failure, and all have appealed to the government for subsidies. In addition to these familiar cases, many healthy companies receive government aid without asking, merely by being part of any industry that gains the sympathy of the State. When the State sets up programs to aid an entire industry, everyone involved is aided. Crop support prices, acreage allotments, low-interest home loans, milk support prices, government contracts for ailing industries, small business loans, grants to companies deemed injured by foreign competition, subsidies for minority businesses, government stockpiling of commodities and foodstuffs; all are examples of the largess government extends to help those faltering industries whose existence is deemed to be in the best interest of the country.

The argument is that certain industries employ so many people and are so critical to the entire economy that they must not be allowed to fail. It is said to be better to take money from consumers through taxes and inflation in order to subsidize the ailing company, than to allow it to fail. Most Americans take it for granted that ailing businesses should sometimes be subsidized. Who is helped and who is hurt? Let's look at the basic issues.

There is usually only one reason a subsidy is necessary. Individuals like you and I have been offered a product or service, and we have said, "No, we value other things more." The company applying for the subsidy is saying, in effect, "That individual over there does not want to pay my price for my product. Since he will not buy my product voluntarily, I demand that you take his money by force and give it to me. His judgment is faulty, and it will be in his best interest if he is forced to buy my goods."

A corporation that fails in the marketplace would not be willing to come directly to you and force you to buy at the point of a gun. After all, that is both illegal and dangerous. Yet that is exactly what is being done under the guise of government subsidy—only this time the government is holding the gun, and the theft is called "legal", and "in the national interest."

Remember now, the government has no money of its own. It produces no wealth. Everything it has it takes from individuals who are producers. It takes through taxes, or by deficit spending. Therefore, what it gives in subsidy, it must first take from a producer or a saver. Subsidies are plunder.

Perhaps just pointing out that you are being ripped off by subsidies has not answered the central question. In certain cases, might subsidies still be beneficial to the nation as a whole?

No. They do benefit some individuals in the short term (those who receive the subsidies), but they do so at the expense of all the others. In the long run, even those who receive subsidies are hurt. Let me demonstrate.

You and Maynard are on your island again. You are producing fish, and he is producing bread. One day another person is cast up on your shores, and he turns out to be an accomplished breadmaker. He looks over your little economy, and decides to put his skills to work. He begins producing bread. He is not as fastidious as Maynard, taking less care in gathering his grain, and spending little time in cleaning up his bakery, but he is fast, and manages to turn out four loaves per day. He immediately offers to trade you *two* loaves for a fish. You look over his product. You recognize that its quality is lower than Maynard's, but still it is two loaves instead of one. You take him up on his offer.

Maynard is dismayed. He can continue to produce bread, but if he wants to trade it for fish, he'll have to compete with the new baker's price, that is, a loaf for half a fish, or two loaves for one whole fish. This reduces his standard of living relative to yours and the other baker's. You and the other baker now each can consume one fish and two loaves of bread per day. Maynard now only has two loaves of bread and no fish.

Maynard demands that the two of you share your new affluence. He wants you each to give him one-third of a fish, while he keeps both his loaves of bread. That way all three of you will have an equal standard of living. Maynard demands this on the basis that he has been injured by the efficiency of the new baker.

If you subsidize Maynard, it reduces your standard of living while increasing his. There is absolutely no benefit to you from the subsidy. Even if Maynard goes completely out of business and stops making bread altogether, it does not affect you or the new baker. You both still enjoy the same higher standard of living. When Maynard stops producing, it only hurts Maynard.

You point out to Maynard that if his inefficiency relative to the other baker justifies half a fish as subsidy, you would be justified in getting an even greater subsidy were you to switch to breadmaking, since you are even less efficient than he as a baker. When you tried breadmaking, you could only produce one loaf each day. By claiming he is injured by the efficiency of the newcomer, Maynard is really attempting to penalize you for his own lack of competence.

If you do not subsidize Maynard, he will be forced to either subsist on his lower standard of living, increase his efficiency by working harder to produce more bread, or search around for another product to produce that will be appealing to both of you. In other words, he either eats less, produces more, or produces something else. Your refusal to subsidize him is a direct incentive for Maynard to be more productive. If he rises to the challenge, which human nature will force him to do, the whole society will be better off. The GNP of your little society is now eight units of production (two fish from you, four loaves of bread from the new baker, and two from Maynard). If Maynard increases his production, the GNP rises. He will be the first to benefit. But if his production goes even higher, eventually the increased production will be spread around through price adjustments.

Members of an ailing industry claim they have been damaged because others will no longer pay them enough for their products. They also claim that if they do not receive a subsidy, they will not be able to buy the products of others, and everyone will be hurt. Just the opposite is true. If a producer is inefficient, or is manufacturing products others don't want, everyone else in society is injured when money is taken from them and given to this producer to keep him producing. The victims of the plunder don't benefit from the wealth they have produced, and thus, according to Law Number 2, they will tend to produce less in the future. The recipient of the subsidy is sheltered from the truth that the market does not value his product, and thus he will continue expending capital and resources on it. Everyone loses the products that could have been produced had the producer been forced to search for a product the market valued more.

In summary, subsidies are simply ways that individuals use the power of government to benefit themselves at the expense of others. In effect, they are asking the government to steal for them. We already know that any plunder lowers production and hurts the society. No matter how big a segment of the population is employed by a weak producer, no matter how many people trade with him, it still does not benefit society to subsidize him. In the case of your little island community, Maynard made up one-third of the total population. One-third of the population would have benefited from the subsidy, but it would have been at the expense of the other two-thirds. Even if one-third of the people in the United States were directly hurt by the failure of a major industry, it would still work exactly the same way. The only benefit they could get from a subsidy would have to come from those who were not in that industry, and those people would be hurt in direct proportion to the benefit received by those being subsidized.

Even more significant than that, the subsidy would have the direct effect of causing those subsidized to continue to devote energy and capital to an industry which had proven itself inefficient, and to produce what people had already indicated they preferred not to have. That same capital cannot be used in two places at once, and the fact that it was misdirected to the less valued products means that it was denied to those products which the people preferred. All the preferred products it could have created are never seen.

Subsidy does not create a net benefit to society. Either you get to spend your money on things you value, or the government spends it for you on things it decides you should value. One way, you are stimulated to produce more wealth; the other way, you are stimulated to produce less. Either way, the same number of people are still employed, only without the subsidy they produce more, and with the subsidy they produce less.

We have been conditioned to think that this type of plunder is justified and that it is good for everyone. Just the opposite: it is bad for everyone. It is the worst kind of sting.

Summary

Inflation is a process that saps the purchasing power of your money, but its effects far exceed that simple loss. As money enters the economy via the Federal Reserve, it creates demand for certain products, a demand that would not have existed without the new money. This draws real human energy and capital away from the production of goods that consumers formerly demanded, and directs it toward other things. Soon the new money results in a falling value to all money (rising prices), and the marketplace is faced with falling real demand. Both the new industries and the old suffer as the economy falls into recession.

Business slump is accompanied by cries for help from damaged businesses, and the Fed moves to create more money in order to prevent the recession from developing into a full-scale depression. This new money creates another business boom, again distorting capital allocation, and setting the stage for another, deeper recession. The business cycle is fully underway.

Meanwhile, the separate problem of rising prices frustrates businessmen, labor, and consumers alike, and soon the politicians are pressured by their contributors and constituents for relief. Price controls, wage controls, and antitrust actions are the direct outgrowth of these public demands. Simultaneously, the business slumps generated by the misallocation of capital place many industries in jeopardy, and the politicians answer the demands of these industries by various forms of subsidy. All of these political responses to public demands merely make the situation worse, as all of them reduce production, increase the federal deficit, and place further pressure on the Fed to create even more money.

Price controls, wage controls, antitrust actions, and subsidy are four confidence games camouflaged as methods to control inflation or stabilize the economy. They are born in the climate of economic turmoil that accompanies all inflations. Like the old shell game in which the con man cleverly diverts your attention while he palms the pea, these financial swindles are covered by a smokescreen of social turbulence. All four lift money directly from your pocket and transfer it to others. All four lower production, and thus your standard of living. All four result in higher prices, not lower prices as their advocates would have you believe. The strongest advocates of these four games are the individuals who gain directly by preventing you from dealing voluntarily with whom you please.

These four con games are the tip of the iceberg. Compared to some other more subtle tricks the carnival hucksters have dreamed up, these four are obvious frauds. Let's move down the boardwalk a bit further and look into that popular game that everyone seems so enthralled with called *business regulation*.

CHAPTER FIVE

REGULATION

Every major industry in the world, including food, commodities, housing, transportation, medicine, energy, and money, is regulated at almost every level by government. Just listing the regulations pertaining to any single industry would take volumes.

In the field of finance, the government regulates (among other things) the amount of interest each type of financial company can pay on loans, the amount that can be charged for loans, the way interest must be disclosed to borrowers, where finance companies can open offices, what their advertisements can and cannot say, what types of securities can be issued, what must be and what cannot be said about securities, who can sell them, and how the sellers can be compensated for their sales.

In the field of medicine, the government regulates (among other things) who can practice medicine, what schools can teach medicine, what courses are to be taught, what types of medicine are acceptable, where doctors can practice, what prescriptions are allowed, what drugs can be sold, under what conditions drugs can be sold, who can sell them, what education is required for those who sell them, in many cases what can be charged for them, who can manufacture them, and what can be said about them in advertisements.

In the field of transportation, government determines (among other things) who can operate airlines, buses, taxicabs, and railroads, what equipment is acceptable, how often equipment must be serviced, the timetable of service, where passengers can be taken, who can operate the equipment, how much can be charged, what attendants must tell passengers, how passengers must behave while being transported, and how much can be carried aboard the transporting vehicle.

In the transporting of goods, government regulates (among other things) the amount that can be shipped by different types of carriers, what routes carriers can take, how much each carrier can carry, what hours drivers and pilots can operate, what carriers can charge, who can operate transport equipment, how old operators must be, and what training and experience they must have.

Of course, food is perhaps the biggest industry of all, and certainly the most highly regulated. Take the case of a simple hamburger. A study by Colorado State University identified over 41,000 state and federal regulations that apply to this common sandwich. These regulations apply to everything from the grazing of beef cattle to the assembly of the burger at your local fast food outlet.

This is a small sample. Mountains of regulations suffocate every field of human endeavor, from medicine to manufacturing, from construction to energy. The government is out to protect us— from ourselves. How did politicians and bureaucrats become so concerned about our well-being?

The Source of Regulation

On the surface, the government's regulation of business appears to be a genuine attempt at consumer protection. The regulations are justified on the grounds that they protect us from greed, ensure open competition in the marketplace, and protect our domestic economy. While there is a growing feeling that many government regulations are stifling business because of the inefficiency of the bureaucracy, still, *almost everyone is for them in principle.* But that is a part of every good sting. The victim must be totally convinced that he is benefiting even as he is being robbed.

In our discussion of human nature and economics in Chapter One, we concluded that the only reason individuals take action is because they believe they will get something they want by taking that action. People in general are not altruists. Yet it would seem that there must be some self-sacrificing individuals who are willing to devote their lives to designing regulations to protect us from greedy businessmen who would sell us shoddy or dangerous products. After all, how could a politician benefit from supporting business regulation? It must be that he has a genuine concern for the safety and well-being of the public. Otherwise, why would he work so hard to pass so many laws regulating business?

It's simple. Politicians who support business regulation are not doing so because of deep-seated concern for public safety—they are merely meeting the demands of lobbyists who are hired and paid by businessmen. With only a few exceptions, the entire body of government regulations applying to business in the world today was designed and created *by the very businessmen who are being regulated.* These are self-imposed restrictions. However, do not think for a moment that these businessmen are altruists. These regulations are not aimed at them; they are aimed at *you.* Business regulation is the cleverest of all methods ever devised for taking money from you without your knowledge.

Sound far-fetched? Of course it does. We have been programmed our entire lives to believe that the government acts in the interest of the individual. We believe it is one giant consumer protection agency. In fact, it is nothing of the kind. It is one giant agency programmed to protect the business interests of established firms at the expense of the individual consumer.

For a clarification of how business benefits from regulation, let's visit our island again. Remember that Maynard's business was put into jeopardy by the arrival of another baker. That baker was more efficient and therefore able to sell you bread at a lower price than Maynard. We left Maynard with three choices: lower his standard of living, become a more efficient baker and thus compete, or go into another line of work.

Suppose Maynard is not satisfied with these three alternatives, and thinks of another way. At this point, allow me the literary license to introduce a fourth inhabitant on our island. This fourth person is a judge and policeman whose sole job it is to maintain the safety of the other three inhabitants. He first decides what he thinks is in their best interest, and then uses brute force to make them comply. Maynard appeals to this burly fellow on the following grounds:

"This new baker," says Maynard, "has begun producing bread and trading it for fish. Although the fisherman is buying this bread, he doesn't realize that the bread is inferior, and possibly a hazard to his health. The baker has poor facilities, unsanitary working conditions, and uses inferior ingredients. It is your job to protect the fisherman from his own ignorance, and see to it that the baker does not sell any bread that is not safe for consumption. My only interest is to see that the fisherman is protected. Since I have expertise in this area, I'd be happy to draw up a set of criteria which would ensure that any bread baked by this baker or anyone else, including myself, would be perfectly safe."

The policeman, happy to have some help in his difficult job, agrees to Maynard's suggestions, and has Maynard draw up the plans. Strangely enough, Maynard's facilities and baking practices already completely conform to the new standards.

The next afternoon you trek over to the baker's, fish in hand, to get your two loaves of bread.

"Sorry," says the baker when you ask for the bread, "from now on I can only let you have one loaf for a fish."

"What happened?" you ask.

"Well, the policeman said my premises were unsafe, and I had to spend most of the day building new ovens. He tells me I must use better grain, which is harder to find, so I have to spend more time gathering it. Also, I am told I must keep this place cleaner. Again, that takes time. I only have time to make two loaves a day now, so I can only give you one."

You have been protected, even though you did not ask to be, and Maynard is no longer forced to change his ways. He can continue charging the same price for his bread, content in the knowledge that competition will not undercut him. He can also take credit for being a good citizen, for hasn't he looked out for your best interests without even being asked?

Of course, Maynard's values regarding the quality of bread have been substituted for yours. The bread you were willing to accept has been removed from the market and replaced with a better bread (according to him). Before you had two loaves of bread, and now you have one. Your standard of living has fallen by one loaf, but isn't that loaf a better one? You still have the same total value, according to Maynard and the policeman. If you value the two loaves of lower-quality bread more than the one loaf of higher-quality bread, you must be wrong, right? Wrong. Remember Economic Law Number 5: Value is not absolute; it is merely the subjective judgment of the person making the choice. You are the only one who can decide what you value more, fewer loaves of higher-quality bread, or more loaves of lower-quality bread. Maynard and the policeman have no basis on which to make that judgment for you. It is your fish, and you should be free to choose.

Maynard has done with feigned altruism what he could not accomplish through competition. He could not convince you to buy his higher-quality bread at his price, so he used indirect force to remove the other bread from the market. Now you have no choice. He could have accomplished the same thing by just coming into your hut and stealing the extra loaf when you were away, couldn't he? In effect, that is just what he has done. Against your will and without your consent, he has lowered your standard of living.

In real life, there are three ways that a businessman can limit his competition and thus gain your business by default: first, he can get the government to prevent the competitor from offering products at all; second, he can get the government to force the competitor to raise his price; and third, he can get the government to force his competitors' costs up, thus indirectly forcing up the price.

All three of these methods are widespread confidence games that have been around for centuries. By getting government to limit the introduction of competitive products into the marketplace, any businessman can set his own prices for the same products much higher and you will buy from him without suspecting that he has forced you to do so.

If you still question this analysis, examine the evidence. Take some time and research the records regarding which individuals lobbied for regulations, designed the regulations, and reported violations of the regulations. Time after time, you'll find that it was not wounded consumers who were responsible but businesses already active in the market. Established airlines lobbied for creation of the Civil Aeronautics Board, volunteered to draft regulations governing airlines, and then screamed when deregulation was mentioned. Established banks lobbied for establishment of the Federal Reserve. Established trucking firms demanded regulation of interstate trucking; established shipping firms demanded regulation of ocean freight; established railroads demanded regulation of the rails. Established firms do not like competition. It threatens to take away their customers, and lower their profits. Free enterprise is a fine concept when a businessman wants to complain about government interference in his own affairs, but when competition threatens his markets he is quick to point the political guns at his adversary.

When the entrenched firms succeed in getting the government to regulate their industry, you, the consumer, are the loser. You are not protected by these regulations; you are denied the chance to buy the product of someone who might have been willing to offer you a lower price or a different quality. You are deprived of your chance to set your own values on goods. Let's take a look at some of the specific ways producers can control your ability to choose.

Tariffs

When a manufacturer is threatened by foreign competition, he pleads with the politicians for help. He points out that foreign firms are selling their products in this country at substantially less than he is able to charge for his. Consequently, dollars are flowing out of the country, providing jobs overseas, and costing jobs here. The foreign country is strengthened and America weakened. Feigning concern for the "national interest," the manufacturer asks that the government limit the amount of products his foreign competitors can bring into the country, fix the price at which they can be sold, or tax those products so that their price is raised up to or above the domestic manufacturers' prices. On the surface, the argument for restricting imports seems sound, and most people fall for it. In fact, it is a very sophisticated lie, and you would be very much in the minority if you had ever discovered the fallacy. To understand why these arguments are totally fraudulent, let us return briefly to the imaginary island.

You have decided to build yourself a cabin, and have fashioned yourself an axe and are proceeding to hew planks from trees you have cut down. Each plank requires enormous effort on your part, taking fifteen days to make. In addition, your axe is continually being dulled by the work, and you must take time out to sharpen it. Maynard, your economist neighbor, has watched your efforts with interest, and wholeheartedly approves. He sees this labor as a fine example of an economy in full employment.

One day, as you are laboring away, you glance down at the beach and notice an object has been cast up by the waves. On looking closely, you see it is a plank, perfect in every respect, exactly the type you have been laboring so hard to make. You yell out your good fortune to Maynard, and run down to pick it up.

Maynard thinks for a moment, and then shakes his head

violently. "Absolutely not," he shouts. "Leave it alone. Or better yet, throw it back into the waves!"

You're dumbfounded. "What in heaven's name are you talking about? It's a perfect plank. It'll save me fifteen days' work."

"Exactly," says Maynard. "Don't you see that if you make a plank with your axe instead, it will *provide you with fifteen days work*. If you use that plank from the sea, you'll be unemployed fifteen days sooner. Labor is wealth, and you would put yourself out of work completely if you picked up every plank you saw floating in on the waves. Actually, you can increase your employment if you take the trouble to cast the plank back into the sea."*

I do not have to repeat what you say to Maynard at this point, for his logic is so twisted that even a person unschooled in economics has no difficulty seeing the absurdity of his suggestion. Throw away a perfectly good plank, and then have to go to the trouble to spend fifteen days making one?

Every individual can see the fallacy clearly when it applies directly to him, but somehow, when it applies to the individuals comprising a nation, the fallacy is obscured. Maynard's distorted logic is exactly the logic being used by any nation that imposes tariffs or restrictions on inexpensive foreign goods. Those people who favor tariffs are casting back the plank that can be had for a small amount of effort, and prefer instead to expend a great deal more labor making one. They stop low-cost foreign imports at their borders in order to provide themselves with work. The nation imposing the tariff even sees a benefit from the labor the protectionist legislation creates for customs officers. It is like

*The analogy about the plank is taken from Frederic Bastiat's brilliant work, *Social Fallacies*, (Irvington-on-Hudson, New York; The Foundation for Economic Education) first published in 1844. W.M. Curtiss repeated Bastiat's parable in his book, *The Tariff Idea* (Irvington-on-Hudson, New York; The Foundation for Economic Education, 1953). It was quoted in my book, *Common Sense Economics*, (Costa Mesa, California; The Common Sense Press, Inc., 2nd Ed., 1976), and is used here again. It cannot be repeated often enough.

Maynard's suggestion that you take the time to throw the plank back into the waves because it creates additional labor for you.

Frederic Bastiat pointed out that the confusion about tariffs stems from observing that which is seen, and ignoring that which is not seen. What Maynard saw was that you would lose your job if you picked up free planks rather than creating them yourself. What he did not see was that the same amount of effort that would have been expended shaping the plank could have been put to some other use. By taking the free plank and then spending fifteen days building a chair, you would have both the enjoyment that the plank provides by helping to complete your cabin fifteen days earlier, and a chair to sit in as well.

The jobs lost when low-cost imports compete with high-cost domestic products are highly visible. We watch as the factories close down and the workers are laid off. What is not seen is that the individuals who buy the low-cost products, that is, you and I, have money left over that we now can spend on other things, and other manufacturers and laborers will find employment meeting our demands. Those unemployed workers will find job opportunities with firms making other goods.

A tariff raises the cost of the import and the domestic worker keeps his job, but there is no net benefit to the country. Wealth is merely transferred from one citizen, the consumer, to another citizen, the protected worker. The country is worse off in that it has lost a good plank that would have increased the overall standard of living of its inhabitants.

A second fallacy buried in this argument for tariffs is that money spent with foreigners is somehow lost to us. If we were still bartering goods for goods, it would be immediately obvious that exchanging one good for another good could not hurt either nation. If I grow a bushel of wheat and exchange it with a foreigner for a shirt, both of us have benefited by the trade. Neither nation has less than it started with. Once money is involved in the trade, however, it becomes more difficult to reason out the end result. If you think about it for just a moment, you must realize that money is only paper, and giving it away for real goods must help the nation that receives the real goods. If the United States could print up enough money to buy all the goods produced in the rest of the world (assuming the other countries would be stupid enough to sell), we would have all their goods and they would have only paper. How could we be hurt by this?

In reality, money which goes to the foreign manufacturer is not lost to our economy. We don't get to keep their goods for merely the cost of a little paper and ink. Those dollar bills are merely claim checks, and foreigners cannot benefit from them until they turn them in for real wealth. When they decide to turn in those claims, they will bid for products we are manufacturing, and the money will provide employment for domestic workers once again.

It is easy to see, however, why politicians so willingly set up import restrictions. If the American shoe manufacturers, for example, are put out of business by foreign competition, they stand to lose millions of dollars. Each employee of those companies stands to have his income terminated, forcing him to find another job, which may even mean learning another skill. These companies and employees can afford to spend great sums reaching the politicians and lobbying for the tariffs. You and I may not even realize we are being forced to pay a higher price for a pair of shoes, and even if we do realize this, how much time and effort are we willing to spend lobbying in hopes we might save $10 on those shoes? Next to none, and so the politician hears only the voices of the domestic shoemakers. He buys their campaign contributions and their votes with import restrictions.

When any individual, foreign or domestic, produces something more economically, and offers it to you at a lower price than someone else, you are the direct beneficiary of his skill. Even if a foreign government steals money from its own citizens and subsidizes certain of its industries so that they can afford to dump products in our country at below cost, you are not a loser; you are the direct beneficiary of their stupidity.

Just in case you still have any doubts about this, pretend for a moment that you have discovered a magic wand that can create bread out of thin air. Would you say that mankind would be better off or worse off? Obviously, it would end hunger for all time, and raise everyone's standard of living. All the human energy and capital now expended on the production of bread could be diverted into the production of some other product, increasing the variety and amount of goods we all enjoy. But not everyone would be happy. The bakers in the world would rebel, and would claim it was putting them out of business. They would petition the politicians to pass laws prohibiting people from accepting this free bread. Meanwhile, since the demand for wheat would fall sharply, the wheat farmers would demand subsidies, insisting that the government force you to pay taxes to buy their wheat, even if you do not want it. To farmers and bakers, the magic wand would be an evil competitor.

Would you recommend destroying the magic wand to save their jobs? How would this differ from having a foreign country offer any product absolutely free to your country? Or at any price lower than what it costs you to make it? Obviously, the standard of living of any country rises whenever the inhabitants of another country are willing to supply products to it at a cost lower than the local cost of production.

Some people agree that tariffs and other import restrictions are bad for some products, but argue that if imports affect a big industry, such as the automobile industry, then the great number of jobs threatened justifies government intervention. The fallacy of this view is apparent if we go back to the island and assume that it was Maynard who was making the planks and selling them to you for fish. You find the plank on the beach, and this time he complains that you are throwing *him* out of work. Truly, you are. Pick up the free plank and he will be deprived of fifteen days of work. Assuming that you and Maynard are the only people on your island at the time, your action is throwing *fifty percent of the population* out of a job.

Is it bad for your economy as a whole? Obviously not. The free plank merely forces Maynard to produce some other product to trade with you for fish. You are in no way affected by his unemployment. You still fish, and you already have the plank you need. Only companies and workers in the industry that is affected by imports are losers to low-cost foreign goods. Everyone else in the society benefits. To block the imports merely benefits the domestic producers at the expense of the domestic consumers.

The domestic manufacturer who demands import restrictions is really saying that he has a claim on your business. He has a right to force you to buy from him at his price. Since you refuse to do so voluntarily, preferring to get a better value for your money, he will ask the government to force you to buy from him. When the government places a tariff on the foreigner's goods, you are forcibly prevented from buying at the lower price. When the government prevents others from bringing their goods into this country by instituting import controls or quotas, you are unable to deal with them, and are left with only one choice: buy domestic or go without.

There is not one whit of difference between a subsidy, a tariff, and an import quota. In every case, the U.S. manufacturer has set his price higher than the foreign competition, and rather than allow you to make a free choice about how you will spend your money, he uses the force of law to (a) take the money from you directly (via subsidy), (b) force the competitor's price higher (via tariff), and (c) prevent the competitor's product from reaching you (via import quotas).

You would not throw the plank back into the waves if you had a choice. Nor would you refuse to buy the cheaper shoes. Nor should you. Do not let yourself be conned into believing that you are benefiting from import restrictions. Any way you look at it, you are being plundered.

Professional Licensing

Manufacturers use tariffs as one method of dealing with

competition. Professional groups have found an even more effective way to appeal to the regulators. It is called *professional licensing*.

I would like to give you one vivid example of how the licensing scam works. This example is risky, because you may close your mind. It might hit too close to your most cherished beliefs about the protective role of government. But by now you may be ready to have some of those beliefs challenged. The example is medicine.

During most of the nineteenth century, medicine was a wide open field in the United States. Anyone who believed he was qualified, or could convince others he was qualified, could hang out a shingle and offer his services to the public. There were good practitioners and bad, quacks and healers, charlatans and geniuses. It was open competition for the patient's dollar. The same was true in the field of drugs. Any drug could be legally sold, and any claims could be made for effectiveness. The patent medicine men roamed the country, hawking their snake oils from the backs of wagons, in direct competition with the established pharmacists. Medical schools were also easy to start, required no licensing, and offered education of any kind to any student they were able to attract.

This resulted in the availability of a wide menu of education and health care. There were many medical schools—some endowed, some faculty-owned, most profit-seeking—and there were many different types of medicine being taught, including allopathy, homeopathy, osteopathy, naturopathy, and faith healing. Naturally, each type of medicine considered itself the best, and each was faced with attracting a share of the market by open competition— in other words by demonstrating to the patient that its type was the best.

Physicians trained at the more traditional medical schools and universities were disgruntled at being forced to compete for patients with those practitioners whom they considered quacks and charlatans. In 1847, a group of these physicians founded the American Medical Association, with the basic purpose of eliminating competition by promoting two propositions: that medical students should have acquired a "suitable preliminary education" and that a "uniform elevated standard of requirements for the degree of M.D. should be adopted by all medical schools in the United States." The AMA argued that the country suffered from an oversupply of underqualified doctors, and that what it needed was a smaller supply of better trained ones. It counseled that the public should be protected against the consequences of buying medical services from inadequately trained doctors. (Just as Maynard pointed out to the policeman that people should be protected from inferior bread.)

During the latter half of the nineteenth century, the AMA lobbied vigorously in state legislatures for laws requiring the licensing of physicians. It was successful, and by the turn of the century the AMA was able to concentrate its efforts on controlling the supply of medical schools. In 1904, it set up the Council on Medical Education, which then ordered a study of the quality of education in medical schools throughout the country. When completed, the survey approved the curriculums of only 82 of the 160 schools surveyed. In 1910, Alexander Flexner, of the Carnegie Foundation, and N.P. Colwell, secretary of the Council, published a report that recommended closing a large number of the existing schools, instituting higher standards in the remainder, and sharply curtailing the number of admissions. The Flexner report became a milestone in the efforts of the AMA, and it has had a more profound effect on the direction of medical care in the United States than any other document in history.

As a direct result of Flexner's arguments, legislation was passed that gave AMA responsibility for determining the standards for medical education in this country. To earn a license to practice medicine, a physician now had to be a graduate of an AMA-approved medical school. As a result of power granted the AMA, the number of medical schools in the United States fell from 162 in 1906 to 69 in 1944. The number of medical students enrolled became almost stagnant, even though the U.S. population was soaring. Through its power to grant certification to medical schools, the AMA had indirect but effective control over the output of physicians in the country. Economist Reuben A. Kessel in his article "Price Discrimination in Medicine," clearly stated the fallacy: "The delegation by the state legislatures to the AMA of the power to regulate the medical industry in the public interest is on a par with giving the American Iron and Steel Institute the power to determine the output of steel."[1]

The AMA could limit the supply of doctors by limiting the number of medical schools, but the individual doctors, especially the new ones just entering the field, might still use price-cutting tactics to break into an existing market, or to enlarge their share of the market. Over the last few decades there has been little price competition among doctors, because the AMA found a very effective method for eliminating it.

Most doctors require access to hospital facilities for treatment of their patients. Without such access, they have limited ability to develop large practices. To have access to a hospital, a doctor must become a member of its staff. At the request of the AMA, legislatures added to the licensing requirements the provision that to qualify, a doctor had to serve a term of internship, and in some cases residency, at a hospital. Since the AMA had been set up as the judge of medical education, it assumed the responsibility for determining which hospitals would be approved for internship training, and since interns were originally considered a source of cheap labor for the hospitals, hospitals were eager to be approved. As part of the requirements for approval, the AMA ruled that a hospital could not have any doctors on its staff who were not members of the *local* medical society.

---

1. Reuben A. Kessel, "Price Discrimination in Medicine," originally published in the *Journal of Law and Economics* (October 1958). Reprinted in *Readings in Microeconomics,* edited by William Brett and Harold M. Hochman (New York: Holt, Rinehart and Winston, 1968).

Through this mechanism, the AMA closed the gate to price cutting. The members of the local medical society were already in practice in the community and stood to lose if a young doctor engaged in competitive pricing to establish his practice. The medical society first forced the new doctor to join, and then set up a code of ethics for members that prevented them from advertising, price cutting, or engaging in any competitive practices that might threaten the established doctors.

If a doctor violated the written or unwritten ethics of the society, he was expelled. Once out of the local society, he lost his right to be on the staff of most hospitals. Once out of the hospital, he was effectively out of business. Thus, the AMA and its subsidiary local societies, through a circuitous chain of controls, could punish any doctor posing a threat to their price monopoly. They could limit the supply of doctors and could prevent those that were licensed from engaging in any competitive practices.

The AMA was a primary force in the birth of the idea that individuals should be protected from their own ignorance by government force. They established the precedent that professionals should meet certain industry standards before being allowed to sell their wares in the market, and every other profession has followed suit. Lawyers argue that a client's well-being could be jeopardized if he is defended by an unqualified attorney; contractors claim your house might fall down if built by someone whom they haven't approved; undertakers point out that a poorly trained mortician might damage a corpse or start an epidemic; even barbers argue that an untrained barber is a threat to his client's safety. Nor does it end with professionals. All regulations on all the different products mentioned earlier were born from the businessman's attempt to limit competition. Whether it's licensing restrictions on physicians, routing controls on interstate trucking, or usury controls on interest rates, the source is the businessman, the excuse is your protection, and the result is a control on your ability to make a free choice with your money. For every regulation, someone is making a profit at your expense.

One of the most consistent phenomenon in society is a producer's attempt to eliminate competition. This has existed throughout history and in every culture. Producers already in a market form societies, trade associations, guilds, labor unions, professional groups, and industrial cartels. They begin by establishing rules of behavior and codes of business ethics for the good of the industry or profession (a weak measure to discourage new competitors) and end in aggressively lobbying for legislation to stifle competition by force.

Labor Laws

I hope I have clearly pointed out how some businessmen and professionals are using the force of the state to steal your wealth. This theft is not limited to them, however. These businessmen are just individuals, pursuing their own selfish interests, and are no different either in objectives or methods from individual workers. It is a great pity that our language has differentiated between the products and services of business and the work of the laborer. In reality, they are identical.

Labor is a product—the time and effort of the laborer. Each worker may be considered to be a one-man company whose product is the output of his hands and mind, and whose single customer is his employer. This mini-manufacturer seeks the same thing that the industrial tycoon seeks—the maximum profit he can realize from the sale of his wares in the marketplace. The laborer competes with all other laborers of similar skill when he offers his time and effort (his product) to an employer.

The identical nature of the laborer and the businessman is even more obvious if you think of the business owner as a laborer. He brings together all the components of a product—the tools, the physical parts, the nuts and bolts, the labor, the capital—and through mental effort causes them to be assembled into a finished product. The people who buy his products could be said to be his employers. The laborer is doing the same thing, only his job is more specialized, the number of parts he is putting together is more limited, and he has only one customer.

The price of labor is set in the same way that the price of all products is set: by competition. The supply of labor and the demand for labor reaches equilibrium at a given price—the prevailing wage for each skill. If a company needs five clerks and only two are available, those two can demand and probably get a higher price for their labor than if the company needs only two and five are available. The company competes with other companies for the clerks, and the clerks compete with one another for the jobs.

In the end, the price you pay for a product comprises all the costs the manufacturer has paid for his component parts, including the cost of labor and his own profit. You pay the lowest price and get the most product in exchange for your money when the manufacturer pays the lowest price for his components.

We have seen that the more open the competition in the marketing of products, and the more freely new producers can enter the market and compete with existing producers, the lower the cost and the wider the range of choice available to you, the consumer. We have observed the way business tries to avoid the effects of competition by the use of State force. We have also seen that established producers find it easier to limit the entry of new competitors if they band together into trade associations and cartels. As a group, producers can wield more political weight than they can as individuals.

Individual workers are just as concerned about limiting competition that would lower wage rates (or take away jobs), and since their individual political power is small, they are even more inclined toward banding together than are producers. Laborers seek to establish clout by forming trade unions.

The trade union has one professed purpose: to increase the wages and to improve the working conditions of its members. To the extent that it tries to accomplish its goals by limiting competition, however, or by decreasing the output of each individual member in order to make more work for all, it decreases productivity, and thus lowers the standard of living of both its members and of society as a whole. It is interesting to note the similarity between the ways in which unions and businessmen attempt to limit competition.

Individual workers are threatened by numerous competitive forces. Young people are always pouring into the work force looking for jobs, and are usually willing to take lower wages in order to get work. Workers from sections of the country where productivity is low (as was the case in the Dust Bowl during the thirties) migrate toward those areas where productivity, and thus wages, are higher, competing with locals for available jobs. Foreign workers seek to emigrate to countries where high production offers higher wages. They, too, compete for jobs, and thus drive the price of labor down. Even technology acts as competition to unskilled (or even skilled) labor as machines eliminate the need for workers. I said that workers are competing for jobs. It would be more accurate to say that workers are competing for *customers*. As I pointed out above, the employer is simply a customer for the output of the worker.

How can a laborer limit the competition for his job? He can do it directly by threatening harm to any new applicant. That is common but is usually illegal and is occasionally even punished. The most practical way to eliminate competition is for the laborer to follow the lead of businesses and get the State to do the dirty work for him under the cover of the "national interest." Using the arguments that the well-being of the nation is served by having full employment, and that laborers deserve a "fair" wage, he seeks political support for eliminating competition.

Minimum-wage laws. For workers with low skills, competition comes from unskilled workers. If the low-skilled worker is employed at $3.00 an hour, he is threatened by a worker who might be willing to replace him for $2.50 an hour. He has a simple remedy. He can take the altruistic position that no one should be forced to work for wages of less than $3.00 an hour, maintaining that it is beneath human dignity, and that anything below $3.00 is too low a wage to provide a decent living. The laborer then appeals to politicians, who, sensitive to the labor vote, pass minimum wage laws. Once the minimum wage law is in force, government will prevent employers from hiring anyone for less than the minimum wage.

Labor unions have lobbied aggressively for minimum wage laws, even though union wages have consistently exceeded minimum wages. It would seem that they could not benefit from this, but in reality they do. If a unionized company is producing shirts and paying its workers union scale, the price of the shirts must reflect this. If a non-union company begins producing shirts, it can undersell the union company, and put it out of business. The union laborer would prefer to see the non-union company be forced to pay union wages. In this way, it would have no price advantage in the market. If it cannot unionize the company, and cannot force it to meet union wages, it can still limit the price differential between products by at least forcing the company to pay minimum wages.

This particular situation creates an anomaly. Normally, the laborer demands minimum wage laws, while the employer is against them, but occasionally even manufacturers find it in their interests to lobby for these laws. A few decades back, the northern textile manufacturers, who were unionized, were hard-pressed to compete with the low labor costs in the South where the shops were not unionized. The attempts at unionization in the South were unsuccessful, and finally both the unions and the northern manufacturers joined forces to lobby in Congress for federal minimum wage laws that would apply to these southern companies. This lobbying was instrumental in bringing in the laws and driving the costs of the southern manufacturers up, thus narrowing the price advantage that the southerners had enjoyed. Who lost? You did. The price of your clothes went up.

Minimum wage laws force labor costs higher than they would otherwise be, and thus subsidize the employed worker at the expense of the consumer. They also guarantee that many unskilled workers will remain unemployed. If the minimum wage is $3.00 an hour, and an individual cannot produce some product in an hour that can be sold for at least $3.00 plus his employer's overhead and profit, then no one will hire him. The least skilled workers, normally teenagers who have not developed a skill, and especially the minority teenagers such as blacks, are condemned to unemployment by these minimum wage laws. The employed workers have limited competition for their jobs by force of law, at the expense of both the consumer and the unskilled. It is ironic that the excuse for instituting minimum wage laws is to protect the unskilled worker from being exploited by ruthless employers who would pay him less than a living wage. Is no wage at all an answer? Obviously, those who lobby for these laws are guilty of fraud, because what they promise, that is, a living wage, cannot be delivered by the law they advocate.

The damage to you as a consumer does not stop with the higher prices you are forced to pay. You are also forced to subsidize the unemployed who are victims of the law. Job training programs, welfare benefits, and higher costs of crime prevention and prosecution are all billed directly to you in the form of taxes and inflation. Congratulations. You've been had.

Child labor laws. While looking at the clever ways in which organized labor (with the tacit support of many in unorganized labor) has limited competition from the unskilled at your expense, let's not overlook the child labor laws. Think for a moment about those laws on the books of most states that set a minimum age at which a business can employ a worker. On the surface, those laws appear to protect minors by preventing them from being exploited. Who lobbies to get the laws on the books? The minors themselves? Heavens, no! They want jobs at whatever wage is offered. If they don't want a job, they certainly don't have to apply for one. Their parents? Of course not. The parents would love to see the child employed! The employers? Wrong again. If an employer believes that minors cannot do the job, he is not forced to hire them. In fact, an employer is eager to get competent help at any age, and the lower the cost, the better. By now you must have the answer. The culprits who lobby for these laws are those laborers who are looking for ways to limit competition. What better, more plausible excuse could be found than to protect innocent children? It is the ideal fraud, because it appears to be based on care and concern for the weak. *No one thinks to question it.*

In case you wonder about all those poor children who were forced to work in the sweatshops and mines during the Industrial Revolution, and who were supposedly saved by the child labor laws, let me disabuse you. When someone is held in slavery, and forced to work against his will, that is a crime. But the laws we are discussing are laws that prevent individuals from *voluntarily* taking jobs. This is a critical difference. The majority of those poor children in the Industrial Revolution were voluntarily employed. The do-gooders who sought to emancipate them did them no favors. Their wages were low and their lives miserable, but the jobs meant the difference between survival and starvation. They were choosing a life of toil and subsistence wages because the alternative was death by starvation. What history books fail to point out is that during the period prior to the Industrial Revolution, and prior to the sweatshops, most human beings died of starvation. Abject poverty was the norm. The sweatshops may have been bad by today's standards, but to the starving masses they were a blessing. Most history books have completely distorted the plight of the pre-Industrial Revolution worker. The real facts are available to anyone who cares to dig them out.

Closed-shop laws. When workers from one section of the country migrate to an area of higher paying jobs, they may be threatened by mayhem (as were the Okies in John Steinbeck's novel, *The Grapes of Wrath*) or they may be kept away from jobs by their inability to enter the union. If the union succeeds in getting the employer to agree to a closed shop, or better yet, if the union can get the government to pass a law forcing employers to hire only union members, the union has total control of the competition and can let in only enough members to replace retiring workers. This situation is identical to the professional association that gets laws passed to prevent anyone from practicing without a license. No matter that the outsider is willing to work for a lower wage, he is prevented by law from bidding for the job. This is one more way that a union can limit competition and transfer wealth from your pockets to the pockets of the union members against your will.

Unions have another much maligned and misunderstood method of demanding higher wages while at the same time limiting competition. It is the strike. A strike is identical to a manufacturer withholding his products from the market in order to force the price up. The striker refuses to sell his labor at the price the manufacturer offers.

There is nothing immoral about an individual refusing to sell something he has if no one is willing to pay his price. It is his property, and he alone should be able to set a value on it. If the employer really is offering too low a wage, then the striker can prove this by offering his labor on the open market, and he should be able to find another customer (employer), who will pay his price. In that case, the original employer will have to raise his wage offer if he wants to attract an employee with similar skills, or he will go out of business. If the laborer cannot find another customer for his labor at his price, he may be asking too much. Still, he is justified in refusing any offer he feels is too low.

The problem is not in the concept of striking. The problem is that too often the laborer takes the position that the job belongs to him, not to the employer, and therefore he feels justified in using intimidation or even force to prevent the employer from offering that job to anyone else. Think about exactly what a *job* really is. A job is a contract for services between an employer and an employee. It is an agreement in which one person agrees to buy something that another person owns. The employee owns his time and his skills. The employer wants them and agrees to buy them. To say that the employee "owns" the job is to say that the employee "owns" the agreement. To suggest that an employee is justified in preventing the employer from making an agreement with another laborer must rest on the assumption that when the worker contracted with the employer, that employer agreed never to buy those same services from anyone else.

If you made an agreement with a baker to buy a loaf of his bread, how would you feel if that baker then claimed that you no longer had the right to buy bread from anyone but him? The idea that a laborer owns the job is identical to the nonsensical idea that a merchant owns the right to your business once you have purchased anything from him. The essence of any agreement or contract is that it is a *voluntary* exchange between two individuals. If you do not voluntarily agree to deal exclusively with that merchant after once making a purchase, how can he justify his claim on your future business? He may want your business, but he should not be able to force you to give it to him. He must earn it each time by delivering a product you will voluntarily accept at a price to which you voluntarily agree. Anything else is theft.

When strikers physically attack "scabs", they are using brute force to prevent competitors from dealing with their customers. Attacking the non-union strikebreaker through government force is no different. When a union succeeds in getting politicians to pass laws that compel the employer to bargain with the union, it is simply using the guns of government, instead of the clubs of the union member, against the employer and non-union worker. It is theft of the employer's right to set his own value on his own goods, and indirectly a theft of your property, for as a consumer you must now pay more for those goods. There is no difference to you if Maynard comes into your home and steals your loaf of bread, or if he uses a gun to prevent the other baker from selling you the bread in the first place. It lowers your standard of living. It deprives you of your ability to trade your goods at the value you set on them. *It destroys production.*

Minimum wage laws, closed-shop laws and strikes are not the only weapons laborers use to prevent competition for their jobs. Labor and management often get together and jointly attack competition when that competition hurts them both. We saw an example of it in the case of the northern textile manufacturers and the minimum wage. It is even more prevalent in the case of foreign goods. When you are tempted to buy a foreign product instead of a domestic one, laborers are quick to side with employers and ask politicians to prevent or inhibit your choice by legislating tariffs, import quotas, or outright embargoes.

Immigration laws. When it is only foreign labor that is the competition, rather than foreign manufacturers, the employer and the union part ways. If cheap foreign labor is immigrating into the country, the employer is happy to have it, for it lowers his cost of production and allows him to lower prices and increase his share of the market. But foreign laborers compete for jobs and lower the price of labor. The union, then, pressures for government immigration laws to stop or slow down the number of foreigners entering the country.

Most consumers do not realize that instead of being injured by immigrant laborers, a nation is benefited. Workers are like small factories that produce goods. Lower-cost labor means lower-cost products and more production. There is not a whit of difference between Maynard's suggestion that you throw back the free plank that the waves have cast up than the unions' (or their politicians') contention that the low-cost laborer should be cast back across the border. By supporting restrictive immigration laws you assist in your own plunder.

Resistance to technology. In addition to the efforts of organized labor to limit competition from other workers, unions also have been the foremost adversaries of technological change. Examples of this go far back in history. You may remember studying the Industrial Revolution and how the weavers in England revolted against the introduction of automatic looms and stocking frames. Even in present-day America we've seen carpenters' unions pass rules prohibiting the use of hand tools that might speed up the job (such as restricting the use of larger hammers so that nails can't be driven as quickly), and painters' unions impose restrictions designed to *make* work (such as prohibiting the use of spray guns in order to slow down the application of paint). Clearly, such rules and laws merely reduce production. Carried to its logical conclusion, if the idea of inhibiting the use of machinery is sound, we should destroy all technology and revert to our pre-industrial condition of poverty and starvation.

When two people voluntarily trade, each profits. You are better off with the loaf of bread than with fifty cents, and the baker is better off with fifty cents than with the loaf of bread. You each win, and production is stimulated. When one person steals from another, no matter whether he does it by armed robbery, fraud, or through the force of government, only he benefits, and then only temporarily. He is richer by the amount he has plundered, but the person he has robbed is poorer. Moreover, the incentive for both of them to produce more wealth has been destroyed, so production falls, and eventually everyone's standard of living falls.

This is why the laborer is really victimized by his union leaders. He is told that his enemy is the company. He is led to believe that he is in competition with the employer for the spoils of their mutual effort. He is taught that the company profits are earned at his expense. None of this is true. The worker is being swindled by those who tell him that he should attack and plunder his own customer, his employer. It makes no more sense than for the butcher to assume that the families that buy his meat are his enemies, and to try and force them at gunpoint to pay more for his beef. The idea that the laborer and his employer are adversaries is one of the greatest con jobs in the history of civilization, and certainly one of the most destructive. The employer is the laborer's customer, and that customer must be allowed to spend his money wherever he wants, just as the laborer must be allowed to spend his money wherever he wants.

We live in a society in which businessmen, laborers, and consumers are simultaneously guilty and not guilty. Each is guilty when he uses force to control the right of others to set their own prices, or produce what they want. Each is not guilty when he sets his own value on what he owns and produces. Unfortunately, all three of these parties are continually attacking each other for imagined crimes, while failing to call attention to the real crimes.

The businessman commits a real crime when he uses government as a weapon against his competitor, but is he attacked for this? No. Instead he is vilified for refusing to pay higher wages, or for charging too much—both purely voluntary market actions.

The consumer plunders merchants by using government action to force them to lower prices (e.g. through anti-trust laws and price controls), but is he exposed for this crime? No, instead he is accused of being the cause of inflation for borrowing too much or not saving enough.

The laborer plunders consumers by using government force to keep out foreign labor or to prevent workers from underbidding his price. Is he exposed for this crime? No. Instead, he is treated with contempt for demanding higher wages whenever inflation rages out of control.

It seems insane, but right here in the United States of America, in a country founded on the principle that the purpose of government was to protect individual property rights, the total power of government has been turned to denying each of us the right to make what we want, sell it to whom we please, and price it at what we please. Rather than protecting our property, the government has become an instrument of almost total plunder.

Who loses the most from this system? Those on the lowest end of the socio-economic scale. Since the laws are designed to prevent competition for customers' dollars, and to freeze markets for the benefit of established workers and firms, the brunt of their effect falls on those who are trying to develop skills, enter into businesses, or improve their positions. The laws block the advancement of every individual, but those with the least power to buck the system are hurt the most, as they are locked into their positions, and stymied in their attempts to advance. What was once a land of opportunity where anyone willing to work hard could live the Horatio Alger dream, is now a land of castes, where each is discouraged by a maze of bureaucratic regulations from ever improving his position. In today's world, it is the laborer who suffers the very most from the enormous pyramid of plunder. His answer—his only hope—for a higher standard of living is to see that the whole pyramid of theft is abandoned.

Most people are oblivious to the fact that it is not the labor we want but the product of the labor. We do not want the *effort* of making the plank, we want the plank. Each of us is a worker. Each produces a product. Every effort that opens the market up to totally free competition, and which frees each person to spend his wealth on whatever he chooses to spend it on at the price he voluntarily accepts, increases production, and thereby increases the standard of living for all of us. Each effort that limits competition, slows work, or removes the reward of effort by taking our choices away from us, destroys production and lowers our standard of living.

We live in a nation and a world in which almost without exception every individual believes he is better off if the mechanisms of theft I have described—subsidy, tariffs, government regulations, licensing, minimum wage laws, immigration laws, price controls, wage controls, etc., etc.—are all used. Each individual sees the immediate benefit to himself when one of these methods of theft puts the plunder in his pocket. What he fails to see is that even as he is pocketing his plunder, millions of other individuals are using his same techniques to plunder him. The member of one labor union may think he benefits from blocking competition for his job, or forcing his employer to pay him more, but he fails to think about all the products he buys that cost more because millions of others are doing the same thing to him.

Conclusion

Price controls, wage controls, anti-trust laws, professional licensing laws, minimum wage laws, immigration laws, tariffs, and all other forms of personal and business regulation result from the attempt by others to limit your ability to spend your money with whomever you choose, or to sell your property at whatever price you choose.

These laws are justified on the grounds that people are somehow injured because you, the owner of the goods or services, are asking too high a price. If you catch a fish, how is someone else injured if you set a high price? Why is someone else's opinion better than yours as to what price you should sell it for? Whose fish is it, anyway? Does it belong to you who caught it, or another individual who wants it, or to all the other individuals who make up society?

When the majority of individuals in a society try to enforce their claim on the production of others through the legal process, they are guaranteeing that their society will have a lower standard of living than if they honor each person's right to enjoy and set his own value on the fruits of his labor. The standard of living of any nation is directly proportionate to the personal freedom enjoyed in that nation. The evidence of this truth can be seen wherever you look. For example, the people of China and India are not poor because they are stupid; they are not poor because they lack natural resources; they are not poor because they lack modern industrial tools. They are poor because they have lived for decades under social systems in which the established, entrenched classes are able to use law and custom to control the production, price, and sale of all goods and services produced. By removing the ability of individuals to benefit from ingenuity and hard work, they have destroyed the incentive of individuals to produce and save. Without savings, there is no capital for the creation and improvement of the tools of production, and without tools there is only poverty.

Legalized plunder has strangled China, India, and most of the rest of the socialist or communist world. It is the reason for their abysmally low productivity, and the subsistence-level existence of their citizens.

By the same token, the people of the United States are not rich because of any special intelligence, natural resources, or work habits. We are rich because for the first 150 years after the founding of the nation individuals were allowed nearly total freedom to produce and control the products of their labor. This freedom encouraged individuals to develop habits of hard work and thrift, and to apply their intelligence to the natural resources in order to create the wealth of this nation. Unfortunately, the seeds of destruction were sown when the founding fathers granted power to the new government to tax and control the lives of individuals. As one person after another discovered that government is a willing agent that will plunder others on request, plunder has grown and the rewards of production have fallen. Thus, the freedom that created the nation withers, and so does your standard of living.

CHAPTER SIX

THE
INVESTMENT/SAVINGS
TRAP

In the past five chapters we explored the numerous ways in which you are being secretly and openly robbed of your earnings. Others are using the guns of the law to steal a major part of everything you produce. If you're frugal, however, even after these confidence men have taken their toll, you may still have accumulated some savings and investments. Assuming you have, you now face the second assault. You face inflation as it waits to sap the purchasing power of your savings; the taxmen who would steal part of your earnings from your savings and give it to the swindlers; the investment salesmen and brokers who make their living off your lack of expertise; the managers who manage the things in which you invest; the occasional schemer who would take your money through fraud; and finally, the convulsions of speculation that grip all investment markets in the aftermath of inflation.

If you are an average saver and investor, you have lost, are losing, and will continue to lose a major part of all your stored wealth to the combined forces mentioned above. You may be among those who have been only vaguely aware that things are not right, and, indeed, even as your purchasing power has been dwindling, may have thought that you were ahead. Even if you could see your losses happening, you may have been unable to figure out how to protect yourself. It's time now to take a hard look at some of the fallacies supporting the savings and investment industries, in order that you can better understand why your only realistic defense is the Alpha Strategy.

Storing Wealth—The Three Alternatives

Your choices of what to do with your money can be divided into three broad categories. You can *lend* it to someone, as you do when you make a deposit in a savings account, or buy a bond; you can *invest* it in a business, or in the shares of a business' stock; or you can *buy* something tangible, like a piece of real estate, some gold, or a pair of shoes.

Of these three categories—lending, investing, and buying—lending and investing are by far the most popular methods used to save for the future. Regardless of the publicity that gold, silver, and collectibles have received over the past few years, the great majority rely on savings accounts, bonds, stocks, and a little real estate as the foundation for their investment programs.

Unfortunately, both lending and investing are fraught with traps for the unwary investor, traps that are so broad it is nearly impossible to avoid them, and that are totally camouflaged by a series of false premises promoted by the investment industry. To understand the traps, we must first deal with the false premises.

The Illusion of High Returns

The first false premise is that high or even modest rates of return are easily attained by the majority of investors. The savings and investment industries survive only by convincing savers and investors that it is possible to earn substantial returns in savings accounts, bonds and stocks. A regular 10 percent per annum compound return has long been advertised as attainable and conservative. This seemingly simple objective, 10 percent compound interest, is not only more difficult than it appears, in the long run it is actually impossible. While a few adroit or lucky investors might accomplish a 10 percent return over short periods, the majority are doomed to failure.

Let me demonstrate the impossibility of high returns over long periods of time. Peter Minuit bought Manhattan Island from the Indians in 1626. Supposedly, he paid them in beads and trinkets worth about $24. We all figure Mr. Minuit was pretty shrewd, and had the best of the bargain. Well, smart as he was, he wasn't smart enough to get a 10 percent return on his money. Had Peter taken that same $24 and invested it at 10 percent, today, instead of having just the real estate we now think of as New York City, his fortune would amount to some $34,000,000,000,000,000! That is $34 quadrillion, or approximately the value of the total output of goods and services of the United States over the next *17,000 years!* Assuming a constant GNP, of course.

In short, not one dollar of capital that existed in 1626 has compounded itself at 10 percent in the intervening period. Not one dollar. If it had, today it would be worth over $1 quadrillion, an amount greater than the value of all the man-made wealth in the world. No capital has ever compounded itself at 10 percent for more than a few decades.

Why can't wealth grow at 10 percent annually? Because it is not being created that fast. As we noted in the first chapter, wealth is the real things that man creates from nature's raw materials. The growth of real wealth is limited by man's ability to produce, and is reduced by his consumption. Real growth is the amount left over at the end of each year that is added to his stockpile of real goods. Man cannot increase wealth fast enough to meet his consumption needs and have 10 percent left over each year.

Suppose man can get his real wealth to increase at 3 percent per year (which is probably still beyond his abilities). That 3 percent real growth will not belong solely to the person who made the capital investment. It will be divided among the product's producers (the business entrepreneurs and managers), and the investors. The

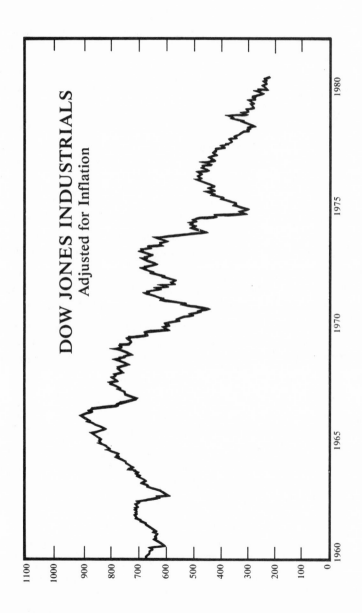

DOW JONES INDUSTRIALS
Adjusted for Inflation

entrepreneurs and managers will always get the lion's share, while the passive investor, the little saver who puts up his money and nothing else, will get what is left.

In an ideal world, one without inflation, business cycles, and extensive legalized plunder, the passive investor would probably find that his savings, when loaned out, would yield him about 1 percent per year. But, in our economy, the entrepreneurs and investors are not the only people dividing up the spoils. All the plunderers that we exposed in the first five chapters are there first, helping themselves to the rewards of production, eating away at the entrepreneurs' and investors' returns. After the world's production is plundered through taxes, inflation, and regulation, after the business cycle takes its toll, and after the entrepreneur takes his, there is nothing at all left for the investor. In fact, it is worse than that. The investor not only gets no real return, he subsidizes the others. Every year, the total capital invested by savers and investors depreciates. Only the mistaken belief that he is really earning a positive return keeps the investor in the game.

Before going further, be aware that there are two types of return: there is the advertised return, and the real, after-tax, after-inflation return. You are not concerned with the returns that are advertised, but only in the return that actually adds to your overall purchasing power. The masses of savers and investors have lost hundreds of billions of dollars of real purchasing power in the financial marketplace simply because they failed to differentiate between the quantity of dollars they hold versus the quantity of purchasing power.

How Lenders Lose

Simple arithmetic will clarify this point. Let's assume you decide to save money in either a savings account, a bond, a cash value life insurance policy, or by carrying a mortgage or deed of trust. In all these cases you are *lending* your money. In exchange you receive a promise of repayment at a given time in the future, and some rate of interest to compensate you for the use of your money. The promissory notes you receive when you lend money are *debt securities*; they might be thought of as claim checks on money.

In early 1980, life insurance policies were yielding 3 to 4 percent on the cash value of the policy, savings accounts 5 to 12 percent, and bonds from 6 to 14 percent. (Some yield more, but usually the difference is merely a premium that compensates for increased risk.) In all these cases, whether you are earning 4 percent or 14 percent, you are actually losing real purchasing power (wealth), because the interest rate you are being paid is less than the combination of taxes and inflation.

Treasury bills, for example, the safest of all loans, were yielding about 14 percent per year in mid-1980. However, the investor does not get to keep this 14 percent. First, he must pay income taxes on this return, which might be as high as 70 percent of the interest. Even the small saver who has a modest income will still pay 30 percent to 40 percent of his interest income in taxes. This means the interest retained by the T-bill owner will be between 4 and 10 percent, depending on his tax bracket. Meanwhile, during the same period prices were rising at the rate of 18 percent per year, so the value of the saver's principal was falling. Thus, anyone who loaned money to the federal government and received a T-bill in return had to lose between 4 percent and 9 percent of his savings per year, even though he is receiving the highest interest rate in history. Even if the yield was tax-free, the saver still lost 4 percent per year on his capital.

Further, most people are not buying T-bills. You are probably saving your money in cash value life insurance policies or bank savings accounts where the yields are much lower than Treasury bills. Your loss for 1980 will probably be 10 percent to 15 percent. Lest you feel alone, during 1979 American savers were lending money at a record pace: they had on deposit over $550 billion in savings accounts, $410 billion in cash value life insurance, and $450 billion in long term bonds. And in every case the real yield, after inflation and taxes, was negative. In today's world, you are a certain loser if you lend out your money.

Common Stocks

Stock brokers will argue that the answer is to invest in stocks, and will suggest that after-inflation, after-tax yields of 10 percent or more are relatively easy to attain. Are they?

Over the last decade the stock market certainly hasn't offered a hedge against the inflation that threatens the bond holder. The Dow Jones Industrials Average went over 1,000 in 1966. By the end of 1980 it was just below that 1966 high. Adjusted for inflation, however, the picture is much worse. *Figure 2* (page 103) shows the value of the stocks in the DJIA between 1960 and 1980, adjusted for the falling value of the dollar. Inflation-adjusted, the average stands below 300. In other words, investors who bet on the thirty largest companies in the country have lost over half of their purchasing power during the last twenty years. Dividends helped to cushion this loss, but after taxes, that help was not enough.

Other stock market averages have fared somewhat better than the DJIA. Stocks listed on the American Stock Exchange have been in a bull market for the last few years, led, of course, by the energy stocks that have benefited so much from the skyrocketing price of oil. Still, there is little to suggest that the average small investor could hope to be in the right stock at the right time, or even if he were, that, on average, the after-tax returns from stocks would keep pace with inflation.

The volatility of stock prices, and their generally poor performance over the past fifteen years is not an aberration. It is a direct consequence of the inflation of the money supply. As an investor, it's important that you understand how inflation affects values.

Volatility of Markets

Stock values are a function of business earnings, and over the last decade earnings have been the victim of inflation. I mentioned earlier that inflation of the money supply causes a business cycle with alternating periods of boom and bust. This, of course, results in erratic profits for business, and makes for erratic stock markets as well.

In addition to the inflation-induced business cycle, rising prices make it difficult for businessmen to plan for the future. Not knowing how fast prices will rise next year, businessmen are hard-pressed to know how to price their products or how much inventory and equipment to stock. As a result, profits become more uncertain.

As a further complication, the businessman tends to count inflationary gains on inventories as profit, when in reality they are not. I was reminded of this recently when, while on vacation, I went into a health food store to buy some honey. The jar on the shelf was priced at $1.00. As I was paying for it, the proprietress and I began to talk about rising prices. She noted how lucky she was to have bought a large supply of honey two years earlier when prices were much lower. The jar I held in my hand cost her only fifty cents, she noted, while now the same jar would cost her $1.10 at wholesale. Many other items in her inventory had risen proportionately. She then made the comment that she was thinking of expanding her little store, as profits had been good.

She assumed that because she had purchased the honey for fifty cents and sold it to me for $1.00, that she was making a fifty-cent profit. I was a bit embarrassed to point out to her that she had not made a profit at all. She would have been better off not to have sold the honey to me, since now she had to take the dollar I gave her, plus a dime from her cash drawer, just to replace the jar on her shelf. She was going to lose a dime the moment she replenished her inventory. To bring her mistake vividly home to her, I suggested that she would be smart to immediately buy the honey back from me at $1.05, since that was five cents less than she could buy it for at the wholesaler. By her way of thinking, she could have bought all the jars on her shelves herself, made a fifty-cent profit, and then turned around and sold them back to herself at $1.10, and made another dime.

Like many business owners, she did not understand that a profit is not the difference between *original cost* and selling price, but the difference between *replacement cost* and selling price.

This error of counting inflationary gains as profits is widespread, and applies not only to inventory, but to costs of plant and equipment as well. Just as a businessman will underprice his merchandise because he uses original cost rather than replacement cost in figuring profit, he will also fail to allocate enough of his income to the replacement of plant and equipment. He may use the fastest depreciation schedule the government allows, but if the depreciation he deducts is a percentage of original cost, rather than a percentage of replacement cost, he will understate his true cost. The idea of depreciation is to set aside a portion of the equipment's cost as the equipment is being used, so there will be a reserve to replace it when it is worn out. If he does not set aside enough, then he must raise fresh capital to buy new machines when the old ones are gone. By failing to set aside enough, the businessman consumes his capital investment, thinking it is profit.

In a world of stable prices, businessmen do not have to worry about the difference between original cost and replacement cost, as it is the same. Under rampant inflation, however, the error is so large that businesses fail because of it. The United States is only beginning to experience high rates of inflation, and it will take businessmen some time before they recognize the importance of this problem.

The business cycle and inflation make it difficult, if not impossible, for a businessman to accurately calculate profits, and this leads to erratic planning, which in turn leads to uneven and unpredictable corporate earnings. Investors, of course, are even less able to understand what the true profitability of a business is than are its managers; consequently, stock prices become more volatile than profits.

Volatile stock markets are not solely a result of the fact that the business cycle and inflation disrupt our ability to calculate profits. That is only part of it. An even greater effect of inflation is produced by the attitudes of savers and investors. As inflation and the business cycle begin to cause fluctuations in markets, savers find that just putting money away in savings accounts and bonds does not keep them even with inflation. Simultaneously, they hear accounts of tremendous profits made by others who are speculating in the now-volatile stocks and commodities. As a consequence, they turn away from conservative savings plans and toward get-rich-quick speculation. People who have no knowledge of investments are found aggressively trading stocks, commodities, gold and all manner of esoteric assets, encouraged by their neighbors, stories in newspapers and popular magazines, and a brokerage industry that capitalizes on the speculative fever.

Lest you think that the phenomena I am describing are something new, and unique to our own times, you need only to study history to see the parallels.

During the American Revolution, the colonies and the Continental Congress printed huge quantities of notes to finance the war. Soon the notes began to depreciate in value, prices rose, and runaway inflation ensued. One historian noted:

> The effect of the ever varying currency was bad upon the community...
> It produced a rage for speculation which infected all classes; all ties
> of honor and honesty were dissolved.[1]

In 1789-1795 France underwent a wild monetary inflation as the government tried to solve the economic problems generated by the French Revolution. Andrew Dickson White, in his book *Fiat Money Inflation in France*, described what happened to the investment markets.

---

1. Henry Phillips, *Historical Sketches of the Paper Currencies of the American Colonies* (New York, originally published 1865-66, reprinted 1969; Burt Franklin Publishers).

With the plethora of paper currency in 1791 appeared the first evidence of that cancerous disease which always follows large issues of irredeemable currency—a disease more permanently injurious to a nation than war, pestilence or famine. For at the great metropolitan centers grew a luxurious, speculative, stock gambling body, which like a malignant tumor, absorbed into itself the strength of the nation and sent out its cancerous fibres to the remotest hamlets. At these city centers abundant wealth seemed to be piled up; in the country at large there grew a dislike of steady labor and contempt for moderate gains and simple living.[2]

You may have heard stories about the hyperinflation that occurred in Germany just after World War I. Money was created in incredible quantities, causing prices to multiply millions of times in a matter of months. Again, investors and markets reacted with predictable abandon.

It was observed in Germany [during the inflation] that the circle of speculators was greatly enlarged. Shares were held by speculators in a much larger measure than formerly, when they for the most part had been held longer by investors, who considered them as permanent investments. But in 1920 and 1921 shares passed rapidly from hand to hand, and oscillations of their prices were much more frequent and more violent than formerly ... Business on the German Bourse reached such a condition as to put in the shade even the classical examples of the most violent speculation.[3]

Today's volatile investment markets merely reflect the natural tendencies of individuals as they react to the complicated effects of monetary inflation. The values of investments fluctuate wildly as one by one individuals learn that savings accounts and bonds no longer provide security, and as they hear stories of the fortunes being made by speculators in stocks and commodities.

2. Andrew Dickson White, *Fiat Money Inflation in France* (Caldwell, Idaho: The Caxton Printers, Ltd., 1972) p. 38.

3. Constantino Bresciani-Turroni, *The Economics of Inflation* (Northampton, England: Augustus M. Kelley, 1968) p. 158.

There is no certain way to profit in such times, for although there may be a feeling that new wealth is being generated, in reality there is merely a constant transfer of wealth from one group of speculators to another. It is like a giant poker game, with players betting against one another, and with the taxmen and brokers raking a large percentage out of each pot.

As inflation gets worse, markets will become even more erratic. Some people will become wealthy, but the great majority will be poorer. Even as you watch the price of some assets skyrocket, and you realize that you could have taken your small nest egg and become wealthy almost overnight, recognize that other assets have fallen, and soon yours may, too. Before getting caught in the speculative mania, soberly reflect on the lessons of history. Prices go in both directions. Most speculators lose in the end. The novice investor who falls for the idea that he can easily take his few dollars and parlay it into a fortune in the stock or commodity market is simply a fool. And you know what they say about a fool and his money.

Can You Beat the Averages?

Brokers are the first beneficiaries of volatile stock prices, and as the market begins to fluctuate your broker's consistent story will be that he can outperform the averages by aggressively trading. The brokerage industry relies on being able to convince the naive investor that he can beat the other players, an idea that seems believable because it rests on the second great fallacy of the investment industry: that short-term changes in the values of investment assets can be predicted. To expose this fallacy for what it is, let us examine the systems your broker might use to foretell these short-term fluctuations in the values of stocks or commodities.

The two most popular systems for selecting stocks are fundamental analysis and technical analysis. Fundamental analysis rests on the assumption that by studying a company carefully, you can estimate future earnings and growth prospects and thereby establish a value for a share of stock of that company. In the commodity market, the fundamental analyst studies supply and demand, and tries to foresee changes that would affect value.

Technical analysis, on the other hand, rests on the assumption that past prices form patterns on a chart that indicate what future price action is likely to be. The technician does not concern himself with the study of the fundamentals affecting earnings, but looks at the price history of a stock or commodity and attempts to predict future prices, based on the patterns formed by past prices. If you are an investor, the odds are very high that you have relied, directly or indirectly, on fundamental or technical analysis.

Investors who follow the strategy of fundamental analysis are accepting the premise that it is possible to forecast earnings accurately enough to make their price prediction valid. Likewise, investors who follow the strategy of technical analysis are accepting a different basic premise: that the past prices of a stock or commodity bear some predictable relationship to future prices. Few investors ever question the validity of these premises. This is a fatal mistake.

Technical Analysis

The basic premise in all forms of technical analysis is that stock prices, when plotted on a graph, form certain patterns that can foretell future prices. Technicians claim that they can identify all sorts of formations that yield clues to the future, calling them by names such as primary and secondary waves, head-and-shoulders, deformed heads, double-tops and double-bottoms, wedges, gaps, fans, and flags. These patterns then tell them when to buy and sell.

Some systems, such as the Kondratieff Wave Theory, merely plot the prices and measure the period between highs and lows, then assume that that period will be repeated. Others integrate a variety of information on and beyond just the stock price itself—moving averages are calculated, as are measures of the volume of shares traded, the number of issues advancing or declining, etc. The Dow Theory, for example, contends that there are primary trends in stock prices, in which prices are moving either upward or downward. In the upward trend, each new high is above the old high, and in the downward trend, each new low is below the previous low. Thus, the investor who follows the theory would buy during uptrends and sell whenever prices broke below a trendline, and vice versa. Whenever you see an analyst draw a straight line that touches the tops or bottoms of the prices on a chart, and then intersect it with another straight line when the prices break above or below the first line, you can bet that he is, consciously or unconsciously, following some variation of the Dow Theory.

The task of the technician (or chartist, as he is often called) is to recognize those chart formations that indicate price changes are about to occur. While the question the investor usually asks is which technician should he believe (all technicians interpret patterns differently), the question he ought to be asking is whether past prices bear any relationship to future prices at all.

David Dreman, an experienced securities analyst and investment adviser, is author of *Contrarian Investment Strategy,* a book that must be terribly disturbing to technical analysts. In it, Dreman cites a number of careful studies done using probability theory on the relationship between past and future prices. The first study he mentions is a doctoral dissertation by Louis Bachelier, a brilliant French mathematics student. Written around the turn of the century under the supervision of the internationally famous mathematician Jules Henri Poincare, Bachelier's work demonstrated conclusively that past price movements were useless in predicting future changes.

Another early study revealed that a randomly chosen series of numbers, when plotted on a graph in the manner of stock prices, closely resembled actual patterns formed by stock-price actions. A third pointed to the parallels between price patterns and patterns formed by Brownian motion, that random movement of molecules in solution. Some tongue-in-cheek rogues have gone so far as to make up charts from randomly selected numbers and have presented them to technical analysts under the ruse that they were stock prices. They have been rewarded by watching the technicians discover conclusive buy and sell signals in these phony "price" patterns.

With the advent of the computer and other new mathematical tools, the relationship between past and future stock prices continued to be tested. Dreman cites a study done in 1963 in which two researchers used advanced spectral analysis on a data base that included seven hundred weeks of price information for various industries in the 1939-1961 period, as well as the Standard and Poor's and Dow Jones' averages for intervals of one to fourteen days over a five-year period. Dreman comments: "All the studies demonstrated that future price movements cannot be predicted from past changes. Without exception, the findings indicated randomness in price—day to day, week to week, even month to month."

Over and over again, graduate mathematics students at the world's leading universities, fascinated by the idea of scientifically beating the investment markets, have combed the field of technical analysis for some method that would work. The answer was always the same. Past prices bear no relationship to future prices. Under merciless computer examination, even the Maginot Line of technical analysis, the Dow Theory, crumbled. Again, quoting Dreman, "The size of neither price nor volume changes appeared to influence the direction of future price movements . . . . One ambitious project analyzed 540 stocks trading on the New York Stock Exchange (NYSE) over a five-year period . . . . The computers were programmed to recognize 321 of the most commonly used patterns, including head-and-shoulder formations and double and triple tops and bottoms . . . . When the results were measured, no correlation was found between the buy and sell signals and subsequent price movements."[5]

4. David Dreman, *Contrarian Investment Strategy* (New York: Random House, 1980).
5. Ibid., p. 33.

Out of these studies came the Random Walk hypothesis, an idea which captured a few of the clearer-headed analysts after the release of Burton Malkiel's popular book, *A Random Walk Down Wall Street,* in 1973. This hypothesis maintains that past price and volume statistics do not contain any information by themselves that allow an investor to obtain results superior to those he would achieve by simply buying and holding securities. The hypothesis thus concludes that charting is a worthless forecasting method. Dreman concurs: "No matter how convinced the technician is about the market's or the stock's next move, he has no more chance of being right than he would have tossing a coin." [6]

In the face of such overwhelming statistical evidence and the complete lack of any theoretical foundation for the importance of patterns, why does the investment community continue to base so much of its work on technical analysis?

There is an overwhelming pressure from investors for some system that can predict short-term price changes. Investors desperately want to believe that they can get rich through speculation. The demand for systems that predict prices is so great that systems are supplied, even though they don't work.

Unfortunately, the same law of probability that proves these systems don't work also says that occasionally some system or other is going to *appear to work* over a short period. If you flip a coin and call it in the air, the laws of probability say that you will call it correctly 50 percent of the time. Repeat the action enough times and there will be sequences where you will be right five, ten or even twenty times in a row. But this does not mean you have the ability to foretell the future, for by the same laws of probability there will be sequences where you will be wrong five, ten, or twenty times in a row. Advisers using these worthless systems are often able to point to short-term results that appear to indicate success, but any person familiar with probability theory will recognize that their "success" is due to nothing more than chance.

6. Ibid., p. 31.

Our minds play tricks on us. When we really want to believe something, we overlook contradictory evidence, and remember only the signs that support our convictions. So subtle is this potential bias that researchers long ago learned to use double-blind testing techniques in order to prevent test subjects from inadvertently biasing test results. The tendency to misread data is enormous when the analyst's livelihood depends on his ability to convince people that he has a method of beating the market. On the other side, the investor so wants to believe the market can be beaten that when a system fails, he doesn't question the principle, but merely searches for another, smarter technician.

All the evidence seems to indicate that technical analysis is no better than flipping a coin as a method of choosing stocks. It would appear that those advisers who use these methods, including those "experts" who write the books, newsletters, and offer high-priced consultations, are nothing more than quacks, charlatans or both. A multibillion-dollar industry has been built around superstition and mysticism. Incredible as it may seem, billions and billions of dollars are being shuttled through investment markets, guided by technicians who are little more than soothsayers and fortune-tellers.

Fundamental Analysis

The fundamentalist studies sales, earnings, dividends, financial strength, competitive position, and other related measures. He believes that stock prices will often diverge sharply from intrinsic value, and his methods allow him to find and buy solid companies that are undervalued and to sell those that are overvalued. The market, he thinks, must eventually recognize the errors of its ways and correct them.

Research has demonstrated that earnings and dividends are the most important determinants of stock prices *over time*. In other words, the value of owning a business (or a share of stock in one) is to enjoy the profits that that business generates. One study of the fifty best and fifty worst performing stocks on the NYSE concluded that " . . . stock prices are strongly dependent on earnings changes, both absolute and relative to analysts' estimates. . . . It is clear that an accurate earnings estimate is of enormous value in stock selection." [7]

The core of fundamental analysis is thus the development of techniques that will accurately estimate these earnings.

Dreman cites numerous studies relating to the ability of analysts using the latest techniques to predict future earnings. The only consistent conclusion that emerges from these studies is that it is difficult to anticipate future earnings within a useful degree of accuracy. Most investors consider earnings increases of 7 to 8 percent normal—and 10 to 15 percent in the above-average growth category. Studies showed that when estimates of future earnings were made by corporate executives, their average error in predicting next year's earnings was 14.5 percent while the estimates of securities analysts were far worse. Since forecasting errors of 10 to 20 percent make it impossible for the investor relying on them to distinguish the growth stock from the also-ran, it would appear that fundamental analysis is severely limited. If fundamental analysis requires an accurate forecast of earnings, and earnings can't be accurately forecast, we are back to square one.

The inability to forecast earnings is not the only problem blocking an investor from stock market profits. The analyst and investor face a second, perhaps more formidable, hurdle. The information that affects present and future earnings of public corporations is available to millions of investors. The prices that the marketplace sets on stocks is the cumulative decision of all of these individuals, each of whom has reached his decision after carefully studying all the available data. This has led many researchers to conclude that the current price of any stock at any

7. Victor Niederhoffer and Patrick J. Regan, "Earnings Changes, Analysts' Forecasts, and Stock Prices," *Financial Analysts Journal 28* (May-June 1972);65-71(as quoted in *Contrarian Investment Strategy*).

time is probably close to an accurate estimate of its real value, given all the existing data. This idea is called the Efficient Market Hypothesis (EMH), and it seems to be borne out by all statistical studies of stock price movements. If a stock price moves up or down, according to the EMH, it merely means that new data was introduced to the market that was not available earlier.

Lest you still believe that sophisticated systems of analysis are available to give you an edge in the stock market, you should at least study the performance records, which are public, of the thousands of professional money managers who direct the investments of the big bank trusts, mutual funds, and pension trusts. Not only have these elite professionals with all their sophisticated, computerized analytical tools been unable to outperform the market averages over long periods of time, they have dramatically proven the point by consistently *doing worse than the averages.* Dreman uses their remarkably poor performance record both to substantiate the basic premise that fundamental and technical analyses are worthless, and to develop a new system that capitalizes on most investors' belief in these fallacious systems. Certainly, in a world in which the majority of investors are following false prophets, the most rational course is to follow a system of contrary opinion.

In summary, the stock market will prove a treacherous friend to most small savers and investors. Although there will be periods of rising prices as well as periods of decline, the essential characteristic of stock prices will be their volatility. No matter how badly we would like to believe that a stock trader can beat the market averages, the sad fact is that over the short term stock prices move randomly. Tomorrow's prices have an almost equal probability of being higher or lower. After taking out the broker's commission, the trader has the odds stacked against him just as surely as does the roulette player in Las Vegas. The long-term investor faces a different set of problems. By holding stocks, he avoids the commission drain, but must hope that the broad economic effects of government intervention in the economy will not erode the profits of industry. The odds seem to be against him here, too.

In a stable world, which we do not have, investment in the profits of business enterprise will be the best investment of all. In a world of legalized plunder that is rife with charlatans and quacks, the small saver and investor should look to other havens for the preservation of his wealth.

Real Estate

For two decades hardly a voice has been heard in opposition to the idea that real estate is the road to riches for any prudent small investor, and, indeed, it has seemed to be true. Prices on single family residences have exceeded the general inflation rate by 5 percent per year since 1948; farmland exceeded the general inflation rate by 2.6 percent per year from 1942 to 1972, and by almost 9 percent per year from 1972 to 1977; apartments and business real estate have had less dramatic growth, but have also shown above average price increases.

Most homeowners saw the equity in their homes soar during the 1970s. Having bought with 10 percent to 20 percent down, and with prices doubling or tripling on single family homes, the homeowner has multiplied his initial capital by five to twenty times, and all this while enjoying occupancy of the house. This explosion in value has presented many middle-class Americans with the first substantial wealth they have ever had. Residential real estate has been rising so steadily, for so long, that many Americans, especially those under forty, have never experienced a period of declining real estate values, and even most older citizens cannot remember when real estate was not going up. Looking back over the post-World War II era, real estate appears to have been the most stable and profitable of all investments.

Since real estate has been rising steadily in value, we tend to accept the idea that it will continue to do so. When we are given reasons for continued price increases like the limited amount of land, population growth, the ability to leverage, and the tangible nature of real estate, we tend to accept them without critical examination. Before you blindly follow the pack and swallow real estate as a panacea for your investment problems, allow me to expose some of the less advertised economic facts behind the value of land and buildings.

Real estate achieves its underlying value because it offers us a place to live, grow our food, work, and play. It is one of the goods we use that brings us happiness. But it is only one of our needs, and we are always weighing our desire for real estate against our desire for all the other goods we enjoy. As mentioned earlier, each of us has limited resources, and we can't have everything. Buying one thing means we forgo another. Our individual desire to own real estate is elastic. If it is cheap enough, we will own a great deal; if it is dear, we may own none. The demand for real estate, then, is dependent on its cost relative to other things. The demand for holding it could fall dramatically under the right set of conditions.

There are two potential buyers of real estate: individuals who want to hold the land for use, and individuals who want to hold the land for investment or speculation. As the population increases, more land will be occupied. As the population becomes more wealthy, each individual may decide to own more real estate for his own use. These things put upward pressure on real estate prices. Rising prices, in turn, contribute to the demand for real estate as an investment. The more that people believe real estate is going to rise in value, the more they will buy for investment or speculation, and thus demand, and price, will rise.

The proponents of real estate argue that real estate is a good investment because it has a steady history of price appreciation. Since an unusually high rate of appreciation in the past is a danger signal in any investment area, we must ask ourselves what has caused real estate prices to rise so steadily. First, have the earnings from real estate been rising, thus adding to real estate's value as an investment? Second, is the demand for real estate really caused by population growth, limited supply, etc., or is there some other reason?

The value of anything is tied to the use people can get from it. Stocks get their value from corporate earnings, and real estate from its crop yields or rent. For real estate to go up endlessly, people would have to be able to get ever-increasing use or profit from it.

The value of farmland, for example, is a function of the earnings possible from the crops grown on the land. A speculator may buy land to hold for appreciation, but the appreciation will, in the end, depend on an increased yield from that land. A study of farmland prices relative to farm earnings is revealing. During the period from 1950 to 1971, the price of farm assets averaged 26 times farm earnings. At the end of 1979, that ratio had climbed close to 40 times earnings. What will happen if earnings remain even with the inflation rate, but farmland continues to increase in price at 9 percent per year higher than the inflation rate? In twenty years, *farm assets would be priced at 172 times earnings!*

Do you recall the absurd price-earnings ratios enjoyed by some of the glamour stocks in the late 1920s, as well as the late 1960s? Looking back, everyone sees that the profits of those companies could not have grown fast enough to justify those ratios, yet at the time few people were disturbed. Who cared what the P/E ratio was if the stock was going to double again in a month? Isn't it clear that the same fallacy is present in the case of farmland?

The value of a house is no different than the value of stock or farmland: it is a function of the earning power of the house over its lifetime. Traditionally, houses have rented at 1 percent of their value per month. Today that ratio has fallen, and is probably close to 0.7 percent per month. If rents continue to appreciate at the rate of inflation, but houses rise at inflation plus 5 percent, by the year 2000 the average house will rent for less than 0.3 percent of its price, per month. At that point, rental income will barely cover property taxes and maintenance, leaving nothing for debt service or investment return. Already, much residential real estate must be subsidized by its investor-owners, since rents do not cover costs. At some point in the future, either rents will have to rise dramatically, or the value of properties must drop. Investors today have bid the price of real estate up because they firmly believe the price rises of the past will continue. This may be a costly mistake.

Also, you can forget about the idea that real estate always goes up in value. It doesn't. Real estate prices have fallen many times in the past. Farm real estate fell steadily and dramatically from 1915 to 1942, losing 50 percent of its value. House values lagged behind consumer prices for most of the period between 1910 and 1948. Furthermore, there have been numerous speculative booms in real estate in the past in which prices have plummeted dramatically after a few years of explosive price increases. History records booms and busts in Chicago in the 1830s, Southern California in the 1880s, and Florida in the 1920s. In all these cases, the same elements were present: a period of mild growth followed by a burgeoning belief that the demand for property must continue to increase, and accumulations of unfounded growth assumptions feeding on themselves that created a rush by the masses to get in before it was too late. Do any of these conditions fit today?

No one contemplating investing in real estate can afford to ignore the role that government plays in the support of prices. There is a complex web of special interest groups constantly pressuring politicians to favor real estate. Producers of raw materials from lumber to glass to copper depend on real estate construction. Hundreds of thousands of contractors and laborers earn their total livings in real estate construction and development. Thousands of banks hold billions of dollars of real estate as collateral for loans. Millions of investors are involved. Tens of millions of homeowners and tenants are affected. All of these individuals combine to form one of the most powerful political lobbies in the nation. Politicians and bureaucrats have an enormous political stake in supporting real estate prices.

How does the government carry out its mandate? The most direct influence is through the mortgage credit market. We already know that the demand for any product depends on the amount of money individuals have available to purchase it, and thus credit plays a crucial role. Whenever the Federal Reserve increases bank reserves, one of the first beneficiaries is the real estate loan market. In addition to the benefits real estate receives from general credit expansion, the government has established a variety of federal agencies to supply credit specifically to this market.

The Federal Housing Administration (FHA) guarantees certain mortgages, thus encouraging lenders to offer more favorable loans on real estate. The Veteran's Administration guarantees real estate loans for veterans, again shifting funds toward real estate. Under both FHA and VA programs, government agency guarantees expand the demand for real estate by helping people qualify for loans who would otherwise be ineligible.

The Federal National Mortgage Association (FNMA or Fanny Mae) is a congressionally chartered private corporation that was created to invest in and aid the mortgage market. Investors place money with the FNMA, and the money is used to purchase mortgages from banks and savings and loans, thus replenishing their mortgage funds. By structuring favorable programs for certain kinds of real estate, FNMA is able to funnel demand into any real estate sector it cares to bolster. In 1978, it began a two-to-four unit program which provides favorable loans for individuals who want to buy duplexes, triplexes, and fourplexes. Currently, FNMA holds some $40 billion in mortgages. This much capital directed into the real estate market has been a significant factor in the rising prices of real estate.

The Government National Mortgage Association (GNMA or Ginny Mae) is a federal corporation within the Department of Housing and Urban Development that guarantees bonds issued by financial institutions holding FHA and VA mortgages. The government guarantee of payment added to the guarantees made by the FHA and VA makes the bonds very attractive, thus siphoning capital into the mortgage market that might otherwise go somewhere else. In the last decade, GNMA has attracted $50 billion into the real estate mortgage market—again, a very significant factor in the rising prices of real estate.

Alan Greenspan, formerly Chairman of the President's Council of Economic Advisers, pinpointed the expansion of mortgage credit as a dominant factor in the U.S. during the last few years. He noted that up until about 1973, mortgage credit rarely grew by more than $15 billion per year. In the past two years, the rate of increase has approached $100 billion annually. Is it any wonder real estate prices have soared?

Nor is credit expansion the only way government chooses to favor the real estate lobby. Farm subsidy programs pay farmers for not growing crops, thus encouraging farmers to hold more land than they would otherwise. Price support payments inflate the earnings from farmland, and thus increase land demand and prices. Federal, state, and local governments own incredible amounts of land, all of it removed from the supply available to individuals, and this causes the remaining land to rise in value. Zoning laws restrict use of land, thus effectively increasing prices on unrestricted parcels. Environmental restrictions remove land from use, thus causing price increases on remaining land.

What we are talking about is "the sting" in action. All of these government programs are the indirect efforts of individuals to benefit themselves at the expense of others. The result has been an enormous shift of wealth into real estate and away from other markets. Obviously, it has been incredibly effective, but what should be seen is that the rising values of real estate are not a natural market phenomenon of individuals readjusting their value scales because of any growth in the intrinsic value of real estate; rather, prices have risen as a result of a contrived, artificial demand created by government interference. Whenever the government uses force to direct funds toward any market, capital is being misallocated. The steadily rising prices of the past decade cannot continue unless the government can find ways to pump more and more money into this market at ever-increasing speeds. It appears that they may have reached the end of their ability to do so.

In summary, real estate prices in general, by any measure, are too high. There is no law of nature that says they cannot continue up for awhile longer, but eventually they must come into line with the values of other assets. The small investor who uses his savings as a down payment on real estate at today's prices is not an investor, but a speculator. This is a role he is poorly equipped to fill.

Conclusion

Government interference, inflation, taxation, unsound investment strategies, and ignorant or unscrupulous brokers have created the most speculative and dangerous investment markets in the history of the country. Bonds, stocks, and real estate are not the secure havens they appear. They are games in which the odds are as clearly against the small investor as are the odds in any game of chance. On the average, the small investor who participates in these markets probably loses 5 percent to 10 percent of his real wealth every year, and if the economic situation in the country deteriorates, which it certainly will, those losses could become much worse.

In this investment game you must ask yourself if you have some special quality that makes you smarter or luckier than the millions of other investors against whom you're playing, many of whom have sizable fortunes and rich sources of information. If you entered a poker game with the very best poker players in the world, assuming you are just an average amateur, what would be your chances of coming away a winner over hundreds of hands? In the poker game of the savings and investment markets, you have an even worse situation, as inflation, taxes, and brokers act like a greedy dealer who rakes in 10 percent to 20 percent of every pot. You may go into the savings, stock, or real estate markets and come away with returns that beat both inflation and taxes, in the same way that you may, through sheer luck, beat superior poker players, or beat the roulette wheel in Las Vegas. But why gamble when the odds are so clearly stacked against you? You do not need to gamble. There is a savings plan that eliminates all the risks and problems. It is part of the Alpha Strategy.

Part 2

The Solution

We should reserve a storehouse for ourselves, altogether ours, and wholly free, wherein we may hoard up and establish our true liberty.

—*Montaigne, Essays*

The best solution is the simplest solution, and the simplest solution is the easiest to overlook.

—J.P.

CHAPTER SEVEN

THE ALPHA STRATEGY

With a couple of exceptions, all of the savings and investment assets discussed in the last chapter have one glaring fault in common: each is a claim on wealth, not the real thing. Modern paper money is not a real commodity. Paper money is a claim on real wealth; a claim on money, such as a bond or a passbook for a savings account, is the same thing doubled; a share of stock is a paper claim on business profits.

As was pointed out in Chapter One, wealth is made up of real things. It is hammers, lathes, shovels, typewriters, windows, doors, walls, pencils, shirts, shoes, rugs, apples, automobiles, and bread. Wealth comprises all those things we use, enjoy, and benefit from. It should be obvious by now that real wealth is your objective. Paper, once it is printed into money, cannot be consumed; it can only be traded for real wealth. Stocks, bonds, and savings accounts, then, are only ways in which to store purchasing power until you are ready to use it. They are an intermediate step between earning wealth and consuming it.

As long as you have your wealth in the form of paper claims, you are prey to swindlers and con men, both those who work through government and those who work outside the law. Since almost all of the manipulation, subterfuge, and theft of your wealth occurs while it is in paper claims, you have a simple and obvious defense: keep your wealth in real goods instead of paper claims. The only safe, rational investment program for the average person in today's turbulent economy is to *eliminate the intermediate step*. Instead of converting labor into money, money into investments, investments back into money, and money into real goods once again, convert your surplus earnings directly into real goods. Simply stated, invest your savings in those real things that you will be consuming in the future. *Save only real wealth*.

The production and savings parts of the Alpha Strategy are plans by which an individual completely avoids conventional investment markets, and instead invests his surplus wealth in real tangible and intangible goods, and stores these goods until he is ready to consume them, or until it is convenient to trade them for goods he wants to consume. Goods to be saved will include (1) the knowledge and skills of his trade, (2) the tools, supplies, and inventory for his business, (3) the regular consumer products he uses in his everyday life, and (4) raw materials and finished products that he can store for later trade with others.

In the area of the knowledge and skills of your trade, it means investing as much as you can in education in order to increase your rate of production. In your business it means converting surplus cash into tools, supplies, raw materials, parts, and inventories. In your home it means saving real goods such as soap, underwear, tires, laundry detergent, toothpaste, and lightbulbs, rather than paper claims in the form of bank savings accounts, bonds, and stocks. If you still have money left after investing to the maximum in these three areas, then it means converting your paper claims into real goods by buying and saving things that others will need in the future; this could mean finished manufactured goods, but more logically, it means the raw materials used by industry.

The Alpha Strategy has one primary purpose: to protect wealth. As such, it will work for any amount of capital. If you have only $100, you can protect it completely against inflation and all investment risks by simply buying things now that you know you will have to buy next week, next month, or next year. If you have $1,000 or $10,000, the same thing holds true. As the amount of capital you have available increases, it becomes less practical to store items for your own personal consumption, and more sensible to store things that you can eventually trade or sell. Only when your assets exceed the amount you can conveniently store in education, business assets, and consumption goods should you consider saving tradeable goods.

The Benefits

There are multiple benefits to the Alpha Strategy.

First, on the level of storing future consumables, you are totally and permanently insulated from inflation. A case of aluminum foil, once purchased and stored away, cannot go up in price; the same aluminum foil on the shelf in the store will continue to rise in cost every year. The difference between the price you pay now and the price you would have to pay in the future is yours to keep. There is *no* investment that is a complete and total hedge against inflation, but saving and storing consumables for the future is.

Second, you avoid tax on the inflationary increase. Even if you earned a rate of interest on your bank account equal to the rate of inflation, which is improbable, income taxes on your interest would still throw you into a loss position. Buy a set of towels for $20, however, use them five years later when the price of the same towels has risen to $40, and you will have completely avoided the tax on your $20 inflationary "gain".

Third, you avoid all risk inherent in the investment markets. There is no risk that $500 invested in tires for your car will be lost if the stock market crashes, or if the dollar plunges on foreign exchange markets. No broker can absorb your $500 by churning your account for commissions, and no inept management company can dissipate it. When you put your money into real things, your reliance on the performance of others is reduced dramatically.

The Alpha Strategy also provides protection from risks other than inflation. Storing consumption items for the future is the ultimate hedge against recession or depression. When your job becomes insecure, what better assets could you own than a roof over your head, food in the cupboard, and clothes to wear? Your real-goods savings account will see you through good times and bad. Recession may hit, your income may be cut off, and yet prices probably will continue to rise. In a recession, you are better off holding consumable goods than holding depreciating currency.

If the nation is thrown into a crisis in which the chain of supply breaks down—that is, if strikes, revolution, anarchy, natural disaster, or even war interrupted your ability to buy goods—then your cache of consumables would prove extremely valuable.

Even if our social problems do not result in a breakdown of the production system, we will still have shortages. Inflation will lead us into price controls, and these will lead to shortages and rationing. A few years ago I would have had to explain how rapidly controls can disrupt supplies, but today it is not necessary—we are living among those very conditions. Everyone reading this book is familiar with the meat, plastic, paper, and gasoline shortages of the past decade, all of which were induced by government controls and regulations. As inflation worsens, controls will expand and shortages will spread to other products. The Alpha Strategist will have some protection against these shortages, a protection which is merely a fringe benefit, an insurance policy without cost, that accrues to anyone wise enough to store consumables.

Benefits, however, extend far beyond the fact that you beat inflation, avoid taxes on gains, eliminate the risks of fluctuating markets, and insure yourself against recession and shortages. You enjoy a substantial initial profit when common items are purchased in quantity. You can't expect a discount from your local grocer when you buy two bars of hand soap. Buy a case, however, and he might offer you a 10 percent to 20 percent discount. Buy multiple cases and you may find you can bypass the retail merchant and order direct from the wholesaler. It's not worth your time to shop around for a ten cent per box saving on facial tissue if you're only buying two or three boxes. If you buy four or five cases, however, a little shopping time is handsomely rewarded. The Alpha Strategist will usually enjoy an immediate profit of 10 percent to 40 percent through bulk purchasing.

Money isn't your only savings. You also save time and effort. Merchants are acutely aware of the costs of handling individual items. They must hire personnel to open the cases, stock the shelves, count and price each item, ring up each one on the cash register, and then place them in paper bags. Selling merchandise by the case saves them time. Think for a moment about the time you spend on a single purchase, such as dish soap. You note that you're low and add it to your shopping list. You locate it in the supermarket, peruse the brands, check the price, and decide which size to buy. You pick it up, put it in the cart, and unload it again at the checkout counter. You wait while the checker rings it up and bags it, and then you tote it to the car, into the house, take it out of the bag and put it in the cupboard. Mixed in with all the other purchases, the time you spend on one item seems insignificant. Multiply this time by all the products you buy, and over all the years you buy them, however, and it is not insignificant at all. If you analyzed your time as a cost, as does any sensible businessman, you would be forced to devise a more efficient system. The Alpha Strategy includes that system.

The Problems

If the benefits of this aspect of the Alpha Strategy jump to my mind, I imagine that the problems jump to yours. Let's look at a few of the things that might seem to make saving real goods impractical.

Not everything you use in your daily life can be purchased in advance. It would be wonderful if you could store everything that you are ever going to use for the rest of your life. You could buy it all at today's prices (perhaps even on credit), put it away, and live happily, forever protected from money manipulators. It would be the perfect plan, provided you could figure out how to buy all the movies, legal services, milk, automobiles, magazines, electricity, lettuce, vacations, and so on that you'll ever consume. The problems with such a plan are obvious. The truth is that the majority of goods and services you consume cannot be stored away. The limits on your choice of Alpha Strategy items are as follows:

Many items have short shelf lives. If you do not consume them in time, they disintegrate, rot or spoil. Shelf lives vary: some things last a day, and some for centuries. Only items with a long shelf life will do.

Many items become technologically obsolete. Most of the items we use today were not even manufactured fifty years ago. Look in a Sears catalog from the turn of the century, and you'll find few things that you would still buy today (other than for their value as antiques). In the same way, many of the things we buy and use today won't be used ten, twenty, or thirty years from now. They will have been replaced by improved versions, or will no longer be necessary at all because of changes in technology. Just as it would have been folly for me to have purchased a lifetime supply of radio tubes for my original tube-type hi-fi set twenty years ago, so it would probably be stupid of me to buy a lifetime supply of wristwatches today. Who knows what technology will come up with? There is no sense in preventing yourself from being able to enjoy the benefits of change just because you are trying to use up an outdated item.

Many things go out of style. In addition to technological obsolescence, we also must avoid design obsolescence. How dreary it would be to have a case of brand new bow ties tucked away, or five cases of hair oil, or two dozen pairs of pedal pushers. You might not live long enough for them to come into fashion again.

Many things are bulky. Since space costs money, most people don't have an excessive amount of it. The physical bulk of some items adds to this problem. For example, it might cost more to store a ten-year supply of toilet paper than the inflation protection would be worth.

In addition to the cost of storage space, there are other costs. You must prepare for the risk that *all or part of your hoard may be stolen*. Less likely, but still a risk, is that a *fire, flood, hurricane, or earthquake may wipe out your cache*. There is a further cost in the event you move.

Once you have a cache of consumables, you'll have to show some restraint to *avoid increasing your rate of consumption*. My first adventure into stockpiling came when I bought what I thought would be a two- to three-year supply of wine. The convenience of having it on hand each time we had a nice meal turned it into a one-year supply. It's easy to use something that is handy, especially when you have a great quantity of it. Like the child who eats the whole shopping bag full of Halloween candy, you may get sick when you realize your cost of living has risen due to the convenience of your stockpile.

Finally, you'll need to recognize *that the plan requires fore-thought, planning, and record-keeping*, and these must be considered costs. You'll need to review those things you consume regularly in order to decide what to buy. You'll need to figure out how much you use, and how large a supply to save. You'll want to spend time looking for the best places to buy, and you will have to create storage space.

If all these potential limitations tend to check your enthusiasm for the first level of the Alpha Strategy, bear with me. I am going to cover each problem in detail in the pages to come, and in many cases you will find that an apparent drawback turns into a very real benefit.

The Morality of True Saving

Saving real goods in times of plenty is looked upon as an eccentric, but innocent, aberration. In times of shortage, however, people's feelings change. If you choose to use the Alpha Strategy to protect the assets you've worked so hard to acquire, and shortages occur, you can expect to have to defend yourself from attack on the grounds that what you're doing is selfish, immoral, and antisocial. Like it or not, you live in a world where most individuals believe that wealth should be shared, that the fruits of your labor do not belong to you alone, and that you should not be free to enjoy them as you see fit. If any of the goods that you save become scarce in the marketplace, you will be labeled a *hoarder*.

If you are old enough to remember the shortages of certain consumer goods that occurred during World War II and the Korean War, you also remember the social contempt in which anyone who stockpiled was held. When people bought larger than normal quantities of unrationed goods, they were confronted with the scowls of the clerks at the checkout counters, whispered or shouted insults from those "good citizens" who wouldn't do such a thing, threats, and, sometimes, even violence. Those who had the forethought to have stocked up on things like sugar, chewing gum, silk stockings, and gasoline while these goods were still available in the stores were not admired for their good sense; they were vilified for selfishness. Saving, or hoarding, if you will, was seen as a trick to avoid one's obligation to sacrifice. How could you share in the hardship of war if you lived fat on your stockpiled goods?

Before you succumb to the emotional twaddle that might be heaped on you for stockpiling during the next period of shortages, let's dissect the arguments against stockpiling to see if they really make sense.

Shortages result from two basic causes. First, natural disasters that destroy goods or interrupt the chain of distribution cause temporary shortages. But these shortages occur because of inefficiency in the marketplace, and not because of the lower supply. There appears to be a shortage in these situations because merchants do not have time to adjust their prices upward to reflect the lower supply. They leave their goods priced at levels appropriate to times when supplies were abundant, and, consequently, demand wipes out their stocks. In an efficient free market, price always rises until the supply of a product and the demand for that product are equal.

The only causes of permanent shortages are price controls. Price controls cause shortages whenever the legal price is lower than the free-market price would be. Those producers who are forced to sell at too low a price stop offering their products on the market.

Price controls can occur during wartime or peacetime. During war, the government usually commandeers a major portion of production for the war effort, leaving the population to bid for the remaining goods. The result is rising prices. To meet the public outcry against rising prices, politicians institute price controls, and controls drive producers out of business. The result is shortages. Peacetime price controls are the end result of inflation, as I pointed out earlier. The government confiscates goods the same way it does in war, only this time it's done to meet the demands of special interest lobbies and voters. The government pays for these goods by borrowing, and then the Federal Reserve monetizes the government debt. As the new money flows into circulation, prices begin to rise. The people demand lower prices, and government responds with price controls. Price controls eliminate the profit in producing, and shortages quickly follow.

Keep this apparent paradox in mind: *shortages have absolutely nothing to do with the quantity of a product available*. They result only from a product being priced too low. Any product priced too low will disappear from the shelves, and any product that is not, will not. If scarcity could cause shortages, you would have to wait twenty years to buy a Rolls Royce, since they only make a few each week. But you don't have to wait. You can pick yours up tomorrow if you can pay the price.

We may pinpoint the major cause of shortages as government interference in the free pricing of goods, but may still feel that stockpiling is unfair and destructive if it leaves some without goods. After all, those who find the shelves bare are not personally to blame for government price controls. Is storing consumables for future use unfair if it leaves some people without goods?

The belief that saving is immoral during periods of shortages stems partly from our religious and cultural heritage, and partly from envy.

We have been taught that selfishness is wrong, and that sharing is good. Parents attempt to train their children to be unselfish by praising altruistic behavior and punishing selfishness. They point to self-sacrificing individuals as models to be emulated. People like Mother Mary Teresa who cares for the poor in India, and Albert Schweitzer, the late medical missionary who devoted his life to treating the poor natives in Africa, hold special places of honor in the modern world. Politicians are fond of referring to themselves as public servants, and protest loudly when it is suggested that they occasionally act in their own self-interest.

The hue and cry against selfishness has grown so loud in the world that even our major corporations spend millions of advertising dollars attempting to convince us that their most important business objectives are a clean environment, opportunities for minorities, and service for their customers. When profit is mentioned, it is almost always preceded by the word *fair,* and is accompanied by an implied apology. In other nations the campaign against selfishness has become a nightmare. Socialism and communism are dedicated to the idea that no one should enjoy a larger amount of property than anyone else. In fact, these systems are based on the complete abolition of private ownership of property, and thus depend on each individual being completely altruistic.

All evidence available to an objective observer, however, indicates that humans are selfish, not altruistic. They have acted, do act, and will act in whatever way seems to them to most effectively further their own objectives. Economic Law Number 1—An individual's primary incentive to work is to increase his wealth—is a recognition and statement of this fact. Different people may value different things, and some may devote their lives to working for charitable causes simply because they value the veneration and admiration of others more than they value the gains they would make by working for themselves, but the underlying motivation is most likely personal gain.

If we really are as selfish as the evidence indicates, and I submit it as a premise without supplying the evidence, then the question is: Is individual selfishness bad for society, and should we use public opinion and legislation to control it? If our objective is a higher standard of living for society, then it is in the best interest of the majority to recognize the nature of the human being, and to allow each individual full latitude to pursue his selfish interests, providing he does not interfere with anyone else. In the case of saving real goods, this means accepting it as the right of the individual. Let me explain why saving is not only harmless to society, but is actually beneficial.

If I am not a thief, and I am not rich by inheritance or gift, I will have to produce some product in order to trade for what I need. If you grow potatoes and want shoes, and the cobbler makes shoes and wants potatoes, you exchange. The cobbler is happy because he gets what he wants, namely potatoes; and you're happy because you get shoes. It is clear that others in your town can get shoes in the same way—by producing something to exchange with the cobbler.

The cobbler will make as many shoes as his customers are willing to pay for. Perhaps you see problems coming later: for example, you feel that there may be a shortage of leather, or that the cobbler is going to move away. To hedge against this, you decide to buy ten pairs of shoes now. To do so, you must either grow more potatoes, which means working harder; or you must go without some other product that you would have purchased with your potatoes. You choose extra shoes over other products because you believe that you will benefit in the long run.

Two things should be noted about this trade. First, by buying ten pairs of shoes, you are not taking anything from the cobbler by force; you are benefiting him. How do we know? Because the cobbler voluntarily makes the trade. He wouldn't make it if he didn't think it improved his position. Finally, you are not taking anything from anyone else by force, either. Anyone else could buy those shoes just as well as you, only the others don't see it to be in their best interest to do so. Either they are spending their production on something they value more, or they simply aren't producing enough to be able to afford shoes.

If other people take the position that you shouldn't buy the shoes, then they are advocating less production for your community. You won't work as hard growing potatoes if you can't trade them for the thing you value, and the cobbler won't work as hard making shoes since he can't find a buyer. The others won't be any better off, and both the cobbler and you will be worse off. In a free market, when one person saves, it doesn't hurt anyone else. It stimulates the production of the stored item.

In an unfree market, however, people are affected differently. If the government fixes the price at which shoes can be sold, and that price is so low that the cobbler is discouraged from producing them, there will be a shortage of shoes. Any buyer who finds shoes at the controlled price is getting a bargain, and would be wise to stock up. If you buy up the remaining supply of shoes, does the fact that the other citizens are deprived of shoes mean you have acted immorally?

Who created the shoes? The cobbler. Does the cobbler have the right to dispose of his property in any way he sees fit? He should. If he doesn't, he will tend to produce less, and society's standard of living will fall. Basic economic law tells us so. If he chooses to exchange with you, voluntarily, how can anyone else claim they have been injured? Neither you, nor the cobbler, nor the others have used force up to this point. All exchanges have been voluntary. However, the good citizens may feel injured, and they may decide to appeal to the government to ration the remaining shoes, thus forcibly preventing you and the cobbler from making a voluntary exchange in the future.

Their anger at you, the saver, is misdirected. Someone has used force against them, and that is the individual against whom their anger should be directed. They lack shoes because the government has used force to hold down the price of shoes. It is the individual or individuals who demanded the price controls who are guilty. The cause of the problem is the price control, not the saver.

Price controls result from public pressure. If shoes have been price controlled it is because the public has insisted that they should have the right to buy them at a price lower than the price at which the cobbler would voluntarily sell them. They have instituted force against him via the government. When this use of force has eliminated shoes altogether, they then turn against the person who was lucky enough to buy them.

Viewed in the light of common sense, the saver does not hurt his community. If any damage is done, it is the result of the institution of government force, and the responsible parties are those that advocate the use of this force. The saver is merely looking out for his own self-interest, and the only complaint that others should have is that they were not wise enough to take advantage of the same opportunity when it was available.

There is another argument against saving real goods that surfaces whenever increases in the money supply result in rampant inflation. The politicians are anxious to appear to be inflation fighters, but they are loathe to admit that it is the increasing quantity of money that is causing rising prices. They camouflage their guilt by suggesting that the public is at fault for buying so many goods. If the public would start saving more (instead of spending so much), prices would stop rising at such a rapid pace. The political leaders admonish us to curtail spending and borrowing, and to save more. They even pass laws limiting our access to credit, and our right to spend the money they so blithely print. To them, the saver is the culprit, and his desire to get rid of dollars and buy real goods is tantamount to treason.

Certainly, this political argument is right in one respect. The money supply could be increased at any rate, and prices would not go up, provided the public could be conned into holding that money and not spending it. But claiming that rising prices are a result of people spending money is to confuse cause with effect. It is the falling value of money that causes us to abandon it in favor of real goods. We spend it because it's losing its value; it doesn't lose its value because we spend it. Pity the poor dupes who follow the President's admonition to save more during times of rampant inflation. He is handing them the knife with which they cut their own throats.

There is one last argument against saving real goods that might be used, and that is that saving consumables diminishes the flow of savings into capital goods (tools and factories), and thus slows down the growth of production.

In order to increase his standard of living, man must save a portion of all his labor for the production of tools, that is, capital goods. It is only the accumulation of tools that enables his standard of living to rise. Any society which consumes all that it produces cannot advance, for it cannot develop the tools necessary to increase production. If you were cast away on the island we talked about earlier, and did not spend a portion of your time fashioning an axe, a shovel, a bucket, and other essential tools, you would be lucky to survive at all. Tools are necessary, not only for survival but also as the only means to an increasing standard of living.

To illustrate why saving of consumer goods is not responsible for a reduction in capital investment, let us return to your imaginary island. Your friend Maynard, whom you trusted, turns out to be a lazy schemer. If he convinces you that certain kinds of work will better your condition, when in reality it only benefits him, then the more you labor, the less you will have for yourself and the greater is Maynard's incentive not to be productive. If he can fool you into working for him, why should he work?

If more people arrive on the island and observe you laboring and Maynard relaxing at your expense, will they be likely to follow your example and become laborers themselves? Or, will they try to follow Maynard's example? Obviously, they will search for Maynard's secret to success. We all look for the easiest way to get the things we want. The greater the success enjoyed by the con men, the greater will be the number of con men. People choose a life of theft in a misguided attempt to emulate the success of the thieves, with the consequence that production falls.

This analogy is fully applicable to our problems of today. Individuals have found that they can successfully use the force of law to steal from other individuals under the guise of "need," "justice," and "the good of society."

Millions of individuals in our society have found that politicians are happy to give them benefits by tapping the monetary system through inflation. This plunder is so subtle that the beneficiaries themselves do not understand that the money is coming directly out of the pockets of the producers and savers. This method of plunder drains directly from the artery of capital, and thus the savers and investors are really the ones who fund inflation. Gradually but surely, this drain collapses the entire economic structure of the society. When the drain becomes great enough to begin to cause major distortions in the economy, the politicians do not cut the benefits off to those who have come to expect them. Instead they try to convince their victims that it is in the victims' own interest to save paper claims even more, and to replenish the capital of the country with those paper savings. Those who try to escape and refuse to retain their savings in a form that can be bled by these confidence men are called hoarders, traitors, greedy, selfish, and anti-American.

The truth is that in a society suffering from terminal inflation, paper savings do not wind up adding to the tools of production, anyway. Paper savings become nothing more than a method of transferring real goods from those who produce them to those who do not. Paper savings only nourish and sustain the disease. There is no damage to society when you or any individual decides to convert surplus labor into consumption goods and store them away for the future. On the contrary, by accumulating things that you will be able to consume later, you have taken the one and only step that can bring an end to the inflation that is destroying the capital base of industry. You are cutting off the source of wealth that has been funding the thieves. When the sickness ends, you can live off your stored goods while directing all of your new production into honest savings—savings that will not be used to feed the vampire of inflation but which can be converted into tools of production.

Saving real goods through the intelligent application of the Alpha Strategy is not only logical and moral for the individual in the short run, it is essential for his economic survival in the long run.

CHAPTER EIGHT

LEVEL ONE:
INVEST IN PRODUCTION

The affluence of our modern world is the result of two things: we have accumulated a tremendous store of knowledge that has enabled us to design better and better tools, and we have saved a major part of our production and invested it in these tools. The only difference between the shirtmaker of three hundred years ago, who turned out two shirts per day, and the shirtmaker of today, who turns out ten shirts per hour, is their tools. One used scissors and a needle, and the other uses sophisticated cutting and sewing machines.

In the long run, the highest and best use of money is to invest it in the tools of production. The more of our surplus that we devote to building tools, the higher our production rate will go, and the higher will be our standard of living. Each individual must attempt to ascertain what is the optimal tradeoff between placing his surplus earnings into more tools of production, or into goods that will increase his enjoyment as he consumes them. Since this book deals with methods of accumulating wealth for future consumption, investment in the tools of production is the most logical starting point. As an Alpha Strategist, you are faced with the choice of investing your money in production goods or consumption goods;

in other words, you can buy a sewing machine to make shirts, or you can buy shirts. Investing in production goods should be your first priority.

No matter what job you now perform, whether you are a garbage collector, a mechanic, an electronics engineer, a dentist, or a corporate executive, you are producing a product and selling it to someone else. To produce your product, you have invested time and money in learning your skill and in acquiring the necessary tools of production. In general, the greater the investment you make in education and tools, the more you will produce, and the higher your income and standard of living will be. This investment in education and tools is the very best investment anyone can make. Once you have invested in an education, no one can take that investment away from you. Once you have invested in tools, those tools will produce more wealth for you. These investments will not be affected by inflation, nor by all the swindlers and con men we have identified. Only the changing tastes of the market and the competition from other producers will affect your investment.

Education

Logically, the first investment that anyone should make is in education. I use education in the broad sense of the word, however, not in the narrow sense of earning a college degree. Education means the acquisition of knowledge, and for the purposes of this discussion, it means the acquisition of knowledge that will enable you to produce a product or service that will be in demand by others. Your choice of the particular product or service is a personal one dictated by tastes, interests, abilities, intelligence, and the amount of capital you have to invest in education and tools. This book is not about which things you should choose to produce, but rather whether or not you can store any of your accumulated wealth in more education, tools, or facilities.

Ask yourself whether it is possible to efficiently invest in more education in your own field. If you are an employee, raising your level of knowledge should increase your output, and your employer (your customer) will benefit from paying you a higher wage. If he fails to recognize that you are producing more, you can offer your services to other employers who produce similar products, and eventually you will find one that will compensate you for your increased output. If you are self-employed, you will find immediate and direct benefits from increased production, as you will have more products to sell, and will automatically earn more profit. Perhaps you can improve your productive abilities by reading, practicing, becoming an apprentice, taking a correspondence course, enrolling in a college, or by simply going into business and learning as you go. In any case, further education is the first place you must look to invest your money.

A Second Trade

Your current trade is not the only place you should look to invest. There are compelling reasons for almost everyone to invest in a second or third skill.

Much of the turmoil in our world can be traced to the strain that individuals feel when their primary source of income is threatened by competition. The ripoffs that we discussed in Part I—subsidies, tariffs, minimum wage laws, immigration laws, strikes, coercive labor laws—are all rooted in individuals' desires to prevent competition from depriving them of their livelihood.

If you choose not to attack your competition through the sword of government (and I hope that I have convinced you of the short-sightedness of using force against your competitor), you must recognize that someday a competitor may come along who produces a better product at a lower cost than you, and your customers may desert you. Cheap foreign labor may throw you out of a job, new machines may eliminate the need for your service, or new technology may make your product obsolete. If competitive forces do not succeed in luring away your customers, you may fall victim to an even worse fate; your competitors may use government to put you out on the street.

Remember the railroads? Once proud, and employing an enormous labor force composed of individuals who had very specific and demanding skills, they are today a shell of their former greatness. Those employees who were caught in the industry's decline suffered. Most of them fought back through the railroad unions, or sought to maintain their jobs and rates of pay through coercive legislation. The more protection the unions won, and the more the union member's pay was held artificially high in the face of falling demand for rail services, the lower the profits of the railroads sank, and the fewer employees they retained. There was no solution for the railroad workers except to recognize that technology, consumer preference, and government intervention had destroyed the demand for their skills. It was time for a change. Those who were prepared—who had invested some of their wealth in acquiring other skills—made the transition to production of new products. Those who had refused to learn new skills suffered. Any one of those workers would have been far better off to have invested his money in learning a new trade than in simply keeping it in the bank and trying to live off it.

It does not matter what your current job or profession is, or what product you produce, you are vulnerable. For example, right now the dental profession is undergoing severe strain. Changes in the birthrate, the use of fluorides, and better knowledge of the dietary causes of tooth decay have combined to cause a falling off in the need for tooth care. This translates into a declining demand for dentists, which affects everyone in the profession. The problem has been partially offset by increased use of dental insurance by industry, which has allowed employees covered by this insurance to use dental services more often than they did when they had to pay for such service themselves. But while insurance has increased demand, and thus softened the blow to the profession, the problem is still acute. Some dentists have gone back to school, investing in further education in order to move into specialty areas, such as orthodontics, where the market has been expanding. Until this field and others like it become saturated, they will have some respite. But who knows what forces will act on the medical professions next? Technology could change, new medical break-throughs could lower demand for all types of medical services, or basic biological research could result in discoveries of cures for our major ailments. Even more of a threat is government. Government could destroy the profitability of medicine by socializing it completely, as happened in England. Or, less likely, government could turn medicine back over to the free market, and with wide-open competition, the incomes of most dentists and physicians would fall.

No job, profession, or business is timeless. No product is invulnerable to change. Just the opposite. The competitive, inquiring, imaginative nature of man is such that almost all products eventually become obsolete. We have factories producing buggies or radio tubes one decade, and they are gone the next, replaced by automobile companies and electronics firms. It's ironic that this process of change and growth, which is so beneficial to all of us, is responsible for creating much of the demand for larger and larger government, since in seeking protection from change, individuals turn to the force of law.

When your product is threatened by competition or change, why let the only thread supporting your income and well-being be the desperate hope that government will steal from others to support you, or that your union, trade association, or professional society will be able to drive away competition and thus force the market to deal with you? Instead, invest some of your savings and effort now in acquiring the skills to improve your product and lower its cost, so that the market will continue to choose it over your competitors' products. Or, learn to produce another product that you can offer in the marketplace when your present product loses favor. Those who invest a bit of their current wealth in preparing for change will be the survivors in this volatile world.

Tools

Education is one factor in production and tools are the other. Whether you are an accountant whose only tools are a calculator, an accounting pad, and a pencil; a mechanic who uses wrenches, drills, and hammers; or a manufacturer who needs warehouses, lathes, presses, and automatic screw machines, the principle is the same. The latest equipment increases production, and production equals wealth. The critical advantage you have by purchasing tools and facilities now, rather than holding money or other investments, is that while your paper wealth will decline in value, your tools will not. Once you buy an education, a pencil, a wrench, or a warehouse, you have it. No matter how rapidly inflation accelerates, you are protected. You have permanently avoided the fall in the value of money on that amount of your wealth.

The same logic applies to all other things that you normally use in the course of your job or business. The carpenter who supplies his own nails and lumber, the hardware store owner who sells lightbulbs and chain, the manufacturer who sells shoes—all have an opportunity to stockpile the supplies, raw materials, and inventory required in their businesses.

Some businessmen will immediately begin thinking of the costs involved in carrying large amounts of supplies, raw materials, and inventory. It is customary in business to finance these components through bond issues or bank loans. The concept of the Alpha Strategy, however, is to protect investment capital by taking it out of paper claims. If a businessman does not have surplus funds which would otherwise be stored in bank deposits, stocks, or other paper claims, then this strategy is not applicable. It may be prudent under rampant inflation to borrow money to buy materials in advance, but the investments in business assets referred to here would be made with surplus investment capital under the theory that these real goods would be the safest haven for that capital.

CHAPTER NINE

LEVEL TWO: SAVE CONSUMABLES

Once you have invested as much of your available capital as you can in education, tools, supplies, and facilities for production, the next logical place to put your savings is into those goods that you and your family will consume in future years.

Each individual's choices will be different. Your tastes and values are unique, and your consumption of goods reflects this. To take maximum advantage of this strategy, you must survey the products you regularly consume, and select from them those items that can be purchased in advance and stored.

If it were possible to create a perfect savings account, it would consist of a lifetime supply of every item you'll ever use—food, shelter, clothes, transportation, recreation, medical care—everything. With such a stockpile, you would have reached financial independence and eliminated forever the risks of external economic forces such as inflation or recession. The nature of goods makes such a savings account impossible to attain, but you should try to acquire one that is as close to perfection as possible. Let us review once more those characteristics that we want.

Shelf Life

The item should have a long shelf life. Hard goods such as tools, pots and pans, auto parts, etc., are best because their quality and usefulness does not deteriorate with time. Soft goods such as underwear, sheets, and towels may suffer some small deterioration over long periods, but probably not enough to make a measurable difference to the user. Most foods suffer significant change in taste, consistency, and nutritive value over time, but a few do not. For example, sugar, if properly stored, will last indefinitely with no discernible change, as will raw grains such as wheat and rice. Canned goods, on the other hand, have relatively short shelf lives, and their quality declines continuously over time. If a storage plan is meant to help a family survive a famine, stale food is acceptable. If the plan is meant to preserve wealth, then it is not. The Alpha Strategy is an idea for *increasing* your standard of living. It is a failure if it causes your standard of living to decline, which is what happens if you are sentenced to consuming goods that have deteriorated in quality.

Accurately determining the shelf life of many products is difficult. In our society, most manufacturers assume that their products will move through the marketing pipeline quickly and will be consumed almost immediately. Consequently, they have little need to determine maximum shelf lives with any accuracy, except in cases where deterioration is so rapid that the products might be affected before they can reach the consumer.

Before you buy a ten- or twenty-year supply of some item, you want to be certain that it will last that long, and sometimes appearances are deceptive. Take paper towels as an example. One would assume that they would last for decades if properly stored. In practice, manufacturers often add resins to increase the wet-strength of the paper, and these resins undergo chemical changes over time, causing the paper to gradually harden. Therefore, treated paper towels may become brittle after five years or so. On the other hand, some items that might appear to have a short shelf life can be stored indefinitely. I have a gallon bottle of white glue that is over 20 years old. I have used it from time to time on woodworking projects, and find its quality has not changed at all in two decades.

In the discussion of consumer products that follows, you will find brief comments on the estimated shelf lives of many items. These estimates were obtained from conversations with the manufacturers, and should be used only as general guidelines in your planning. In many cases, even manufacturers are limited to educated guesses, since specific hard data on shelf life has not been compiled. If you plan to purchase a large quantity of any item for which the storage life is a significant factor in determining the amount you put away, be certain to check with the specific manufacturer to verify any figures found here. Because of manufacturing processes, similar items from different manufacturers may have significantly different shelf lives.

When buying any item with a limited shelf life, remember that it may have been sitting in the manufacturer's, wholesaler's, or retailer's warehouse for months before you purchase it. Either check the dating code on the carton, or if there is none, and you are suspicious that the merchandise may be old, take down the lot number, and check with the manufacturer to find out when that lot was produced.

Functional Obsolescence

The item must not become functionally obsolete. Advancing technology brings improvements in design and lowers the manufacturing cost of many items, and the Alpha Strategist should avoid stockpiling those in which this change is likely to be dramatic. To have the optimum standard of living, you'll want to be in a position to take advantage of technological improvements. Certainly, you would avoid stockpiling things from high-technology fields such as electronics. Cameras, kitchen appliances, and other electromechanical devices are also subject to abrupt design improvements.

Since it is not always possible to anticipate technological improvements, occasionally you'll make a mistake; however, just because you buy something today and later are offered a better model at a lower cost, your investment is not lost. The original item will still give you the same rewards and utility that it offered when you made the purchase. What you have lost is the improved features that you could have enjoyed had you waited. If you paid $300 for a twelve-inch black and white television, and they subsequently fell in price while rising in quality, you didn't lose your investment. You still received exactly what you paid for—a twelve-inch, black and white picture.

Design Obsolescence

The item should be fashionproof. Social pressure inclines most of us to keep up with the latest styles, and if this is true in your case, it disqualifies a great number of items for your stockpile. Many clothes, except for work clothes, underwear, and a few staples such as men's dress shirts, quickly go out of style and would be poor long-term investments for the fashion-conscious Alpha Strategist. This is also true of such things as handbags, jewelry, wallpaper, and even automobiles.

You should think about the degree to which your own habits and tastes change, as well. It won't do to buy 500 golf balls and later get bored with golf, or to put away a lifetime supply of gardening equipment and later move into an apartment. If you do make a mistake, however, and select an item that you later find you can't use, you may not have lost your investment. You would normally be able to resell most of the goods you've stored, and if you purchased them at a discount, and have stored them carefully, your loss from the error should be minimal.

Size

The item should present no serious transportation or storage problems. Estimate the costs of storing, as well as the problems of handling and moving each asset. Crystal is going up in price, but it is fragile and therefore more costly to move and store. Paper towels may be safe from damage by rough handling, but take up so much room that storage costs eat into profits. On the other hand, a person who doesn't plan to move and who has ample storage space can consider stockpiling these things without regard to the costs of storage and moving. To the stable family with plenty of storage room, even such bulky items as firewood, bricks, and lumber can be considered.

Reviewing Your Needs

Your savings account will be a function of your family size, your tastes, and your investment capital. If you don't have enough capital to buy all the things you could store, then you'll review your list and purchase those things that you use most often, that are safest from functional or design obsolescence, that take the smallest amount of storage space, and that offer the greatest profits in terms of quantity price breaks and potential price increases. If two items are roughly equal in the above respects, then you can choose the one that is most susceptible to becoming scarce due to government interference in the market.

Assuming your capital is limited and you cannot afford to buy the maximum supply of every item, try to buy a short-term supply of a broad cross-section of items, rather than a long-term supply of a few. Considering the risks of recession, shortages, and so on, you would be far better off having a three-month supply of every storable item that you consume than you would to having a twenty-year supply of some items and none of others. The wider the variety of items you have in storage, the more your savings protects you against the risks of economic change.

The Appendix lists several hundred common items that are logical candidates for an Alpha Strategy savings account. Examine each item on the list and make a rough estimate of the total quantity that you and the other members of your family consume in a year. Multiply your estimated annual consumption by the shelf life of the item. This will tell you the total quantity you could reasonably stockpile. Multiply the quantity by the price, and you'll have the maximum amount of capital that you could invest in that asset.

By adding up the potential costs of all the items you could store, you'll have a rough idea of the total amount of paper money that you could invest in personal consumption items. If you have sufficient paper savings to buy it all, do so. If not, select a cross section of the most practical goods to store, and buy those. You can then add to your stockpile each month from your surplus earnings.

Your Home

The most sensible purchase of all is the home. It represents the largest investment you can make in consumption goods, and the most logical. Inflation will continue, and rents will be forced higher and higher. Furthermore, even if rent controls are instituted, the renter's situation will only become worse, as shortages will make rentals difficult if not impossible to find. Unless there is a doubt as to how long you intend to live in an area, *buy your home*, do not rent.

Although many homeowners have enjoyed immense increases in the prices of their homes in the past few years, this is not the purpose of buying under the Alpha Strategy. Your purpose is to protect the purchasing power of your paper savings by converting them into real wealth.

If you own your own home, you have a wide range of opportunities for storing wealth in maintenance and repair goods. If you've been a regular customer of your local hardware store, you're aware of the rapid price increases on these items.

Most paints and paint thinners have long shelf lives, and could be purchased in advance and stored. The next time you decide to paint your house, consider buying enough paint and equipment to do the job two or three times. If you're not certain of the color you'll choose the next time around, buy neutral paint, and mix in the colors when the time comes.

Tools, bits, and blades are perfect items. Make an estimate of the number of hammers, saws, screwdrivers, circular saw blades, drill bits, etc., that you'll be likely to need over the next twenty or thirty years, and buy them.

Garden tools, hoses, work gloves, lawnmowers, lawnmower parts, leaf and trash bags, insecticides, plant food, fertilizers, and seeds are a few of the things used in the yard and garden that should be considered. Even wheelbarrows and plastic or metal trash barrels could be bought and stored, provided you have room. (Trash barrels can make excellent storage containers for other items.)

All the minor hardware that is used in home maintenance should be stockpiled, as well. Screws, nails, wall anchors, screening, sandpaper, masking tape, sprinkler heads, pipe, glue, plastic sheeting, and hinges are just a few of the multitude of things that the average homeowner is constantly running to the hardware store to buy. Bought in advance, they preserve the purchasing power of your money, and simultaneously save you time and energy, since you have them on hand when you need them.

One item that everyone uses is the common lightbulb. The annual consumption rate per household is twenty-four bulbs, which means that over twenty years the average home will use 480. Since bulbs come forty-eight to the case, a family could buy ten cases and not have to buy another bulb for twenty years. In early 1980, bulbs were selling for between 50 cents and 70 cents apiece; thus, in addition to the discount you could get for buying in quantity, a stockpile of bulbs could preserve between $250 and $350 of your purchasing power.

In reviewing maintenance items, don't forget spare parts and filters for furnaces, heaters, air conditioners, water softeners, and water heaters. Homes with hot tubs or swimming pools can stockpile chemicals, filter materials, and pool cleaning equipment, as well.

Foods

Foods are the number one consumption item for most of us, but because of their perishable nature they must be carefully selected.

To begin with, you can eliminate all your fresh meats, fruits, and vegetables, as they will not keep long enough to be used as a long-term inflation hedge. There has been a growing demand for freeze-dried foods during the past few years, most of it coming from those who feel that there will be a breakdown in the chain of supply. While you may choose to put away freeze-dried foods, remember that they do not fall within the definition of good savings assets. As was mentioned earlier, the Alpha Strategy is a means to protect purchasing power, and is not intended to be a means to defend against social collapse.

Canned foods. Certain canned goods may keep for several years, but over time usually suffer some deterioration of taste and nutritive value. Acidic canned foods have the shortest shelf lives, and manufacturers recommend that they be used within one year. These would include canned fruits such as pineapple and grapefruit, and canned spinach. Most canned vegetables such as potatoes, yams, corn, carrots, and beans will lose very little in food value or flavor over the first year, and if stored in a cool, dry place may last for two or three years without substantial deterioration. As a basic rule of thumb, however, try to use all canned foods within eighteen months. The most sensible strategy for canned goods is to always buy a one-year supply of each item. Since prices are rising monthly, even this limited supply offers significant inflation protection, and the convenience of bulk buying will add to your profits.

Sugars. Sugar makes a good preservative, so any canned foods rich in sugar are likely to have long shelf lives. Jams, jellies, and other preserves will last indefinitely, as will most fruits that are packed in sugar syrups. Sugar itself is an excellent storage item. Historically, it has been most susceptible to price controls; consequently, it has been subject to periodic shortages. The indefinite storage life of sugar makes the stockpiling of a ten- or twenty-year supply a most prudent idea.

Honey, syrup, and molasses are nearly pure sugar, and can be kept for years with no discernible change in taste. At most, they may crystallize, but this does not represent a change in chemical composition, merely a bonding of the individual sugar molecules to one another. The crystals can be easily broken up by heating and stirring. Some nutritionists suggest that honey has certain beneficial enzymes that can be destroyed by heat, so if you're concerned about this, keep the temperature of the honey below 150 degrees when dissolving the crystals. The taste of the honey or syrup should not be affected by higher temperatures.

While on the subject of honey and syrup, most producers pack it in store-size containers of eight, twelve, sixteen and thirty-two ounces, as well as in gallon and five-gallon sizes. A five-gallon tin of honey weighs about sixty pounds, and is usually about half the price of the honey packed in the smaller sizes.

Frozen Foods. When I mention the Alpha Strategy, many people immediately tell me of the money they have saved by buying frozen sides of beef. With beef prices skyrocketing, they not only gained the advantage of bulk buying but bypassed the price hikes as well. Lest the strategy get nicknamed "The Frozen Beef Strategy," let me warn you that frozen foods may be one of the poorer ways to preserve the purchasing power of your savings.

To begin with, frozen foods deteriorate with time. At the

temperature of the average freezer (about zero degrees Fahrenheit), there is still a very slow biochemical process occurring which can change food's texture and taste. Moreover, unless frozen foods are absolutely vacuum-sealed, moisture loss gradually dries them out. The stories about mammoths still being edible after being frozen in Siberian ice for thousands of years may be slightly exaggerated, and besides, that Siberian ice is far colder than the average freezer. The storage life of different meats and vegetables varies, but a general rule of thumb is that each ten-degree rise in temperature cuts the storage life in half. If you could maintain the temperature of your freezer at fifty degrees below zero, you could significantly extend the storage life of the foods. The only way you might get permanent storage without deterioration would be to get the temperature down to the point where oxygen liquifies (around 300 degrees below zero). By the time you managed that, your savings from storing the food would have long since evaporated.

This brings us to the major drawback to frozen foods—the storage cost is high relative to other goods. You can pack about 28 pounds of frozen meat in one cubic foot of freezer space. Assuming an average cost of $2.50 per pound for beef, the cost of a cubic foot (about 28 pounds) would be $70, and, at 5 cents per kilowatt-hour, the cost per year for the electricity to store it would be $2.50, or 3.5 percent of the value, not including the freezer and the cost of the floor space. Even if you have plenty of space and already have a freezer, the costs are still higher than the storage costs for the majority of other items.

Finally, keeping your wealth in frozen food adds one additional risk. If you lose your electric power for any substantial length of time, all the food could thaw. If you happen to be gone on vacation when this occurs, you could lose your entire investment.

In spite of the drawbacks and costs, you may still decide to place part of your assets on ice. Freezers have been around for years and many people are already following the Alpha Strategy on a small scale. The inflation protection may not be as great as with other goods, but there is still the convenience of having food handy, and the initial savings to be enjoyed by taking advantage of seasonal low prices and periodic supermarket specials.

Grains, legumes, and other seeds. Nature designed seeds to pass many seasons without significant change, and seeds form a major part of the human diet. All grains—wheat, rice, oats, rye, barley, millet, etc.—are seeds. So are corn, peas, all kinds of beans, coffee, and nuts. When dried, all but a few of these can be stored for years without danger of deterioration, provided certain simple storage rules are followed.

First, let's cover those seeds that don't keep well.

You can eliminate nuts, as they have a relatively short shelf life. Oilier nuts, such as peanuts, lose palatability after a few weeks, although if refrigerated they might be good for up to six months. Even the drier nuts will retain their flavor for only a few months at room temperature.

Coffee is a high-cost item that is a staple in most people's homes, but according to coffee manufacturers, it has a short shelf life even when vacuum packed (about ten to twelve months). The raw, dried coffee beans begin to lose their flavor in about six months. Although coffee producers claim a short shelf life, some individuals report opening cans of coffee that were ten or fifteen years old, but which were still fully flavorful. If you drink a lot of coffee, you might consider putting away a pound or two for a couple of years. If you open it and find that it is still acceptable, then you can go ahead and stockpile from that point forward. If it is stale, then you can assume the manufacturers are right.

The best seeds for storage are grains such as wheat and rice, and dried legumes, such as peas and beans. All of these will keep ten years or more if properly stored, and will suffer no significant loss of taste or nutritive values.

Most seeds contain oil, and for this reason it is best to store the grains whole, without crushing. Once milled, grains are not only more susceptible to insects, they can also turn rancid as the oil is exposed to air when the seed is crushed. Wheat, for example, will keep for decades if properly stored, while flour will normally last only a few months. If you use a lot of flour or cornmeal, as most of us do, store the grains whole and buy yourself a small electric mill for grinding them into meal and flour.

Care should be taken in storage of all of these seeds, as they are subject to mold, insects, and rodents. They should be kept dry and as cool as possible, preferably in airtight containers. Verify that the moisture content of the grain is less than 10% when putting it into the airtight container, then even if insects do get inside, they won't survive. The same five-gallon tins that honey comes in are perfect for the grains, as they are easy to handle, and are square, so they stack and pack well, and are inexpensive.

A good source for bulk purchases of all the grains are the health food stores. You might also contact the local Mormon church, as they often have co-op buying arrangements.

Tea. Tea is another near-perfect savings asset. In the small quantities in which we normally purchase it, tea is very expensive, and so bulk buying saves significant money. Tea takes little storage room, and suffers no significant loss of quality over time. My Chinese friends have informed me that the highest quality teas, some costing more per ounce than gold itself, grow even more valuable with age. The longevity of tea is attested to by the fact that in times past it has been used as money in various sections of the Orient.

If you enjoy black tea, consider buying tea "bricks," highly compressed blocks of tea, usually about eight inches square and an inch thick. They take little room to store, will last indefinitely, and can be broken apart and used as required.

One of the great advantages of the Alpha Strategy is that large purchases give us an incentive to spend the time necessary to become knowledgeable about many of the common products that otherwise pass through our lives unnoticed. Tea is a good example. In the Orient, where it has been the primary beverage for hundreds of years, it is understood and appreciated much like fine wines are savored in the West. There are numerous varieties of tea grown throughout the region that stretches from Java to Japan, and from

India to Sumatra. The connoisseur will know the differences between the black teas of China and those of Ceylon, or the green teas of India and those of Japan. As tea "tyros," Americans tend to buy it occasionally, a small box at a time, and usually will not spend the time to sample different types or to study the history and nuances of the beverage.

If you save tea, you will be faced with buying a supply sufficient to last many years. What a magnificent incentive to spend a day in the library researching the fine points of tea, or to take a trip to your local Oriental neighborhood where you might find a knowledgeable old tea merchant who would be willing to share his wisdom and let you sample the wide range of varieties. Being faced with selecting items for our stockpile is perfect justification for investing time in learning more about the products we consume, and this in turn should significantly increase the pleasure we get from consuming them.

Other dry foods. Another dry food that most of us consume is pasta, including noodles, spaghetti, macaroni, and lasagna. Pastas have a long shelf life (five years or more), and can be purchased in economical bulk containers from Italian markets, or grocers who cater to restaurants. Storage requirements are simple, and similar to the requirements for grains. Just keep them dry, cool, and protect them from bugs and mice.

Miscellaneous foods. There are a variety of other minor food items that can be part of your savings plan. Cornstarch, gelatin, baking soda, pepper, and salt are a few of the lesser items that can be stored for several years without deterioration.

Cooking oil has a shelf life of approximately three years if it is unopened. Oil deteriorates when exposed to air, so as long as it remains sealed, it stays fresh. Shortening or lard, which is animal fat, will keep for five years or more, but again, deterioration begins once oxygen gets to it. When stocking up on oil and shortening, stockpile it in sizes of containers you can conveniently use up in about six months.

Vinegar is a preservative agent in itself, and therefore a perfect item. The average family does not consume much, but it makes sense to put away at least a five-year supply. There are no special storage requirements.

Herbs and spices can also be saved, but because of the small quantities of these items consumed by the average family, you probably will find that the convenience of having them on hand will become more important than the inflation protection. If properly stored (that is, under dry, dark, cool conditions), whole spices such as whole nutmeg, cloves, allspice, and stick cinnamon will keep for a minimum of five years. Ground spices and the leafy herbs will keep a minimum of two years, while members of the red pepper family such as cayenne, chili powder and paprika will stay fresh for about a year (two years if refrigerated).

Vitamins. Vitamins are one of the food items for which accurate shelf life information is hard to obtain. It seems that the manufacturers have no compelling need to determine just how long vitamins might last on the shelf, beyond making certain that they have a minimum potency loss over the year or two that they might be in the distribution chain. Occasionally a retailer will come across a case that has been in his warehouse for four or five years, and will send a sample to the manufacturer to test potency, in which case some knowledge is gained. Since the samples are random, and the storage conditions uncontrolled, the conclusions that can be drawn from these tests are tentative at best.

In considering what brand and type of vitamins to stockpile, the Alpha Strategist should keep just a couple of basics in mind. Tablet, capsule, and powdered vitamins will have a significantly longer shelf life than liquid preparations. The enemies of potency are high humidity and high temperatures, so the vitamins should be kept in moisture-proof containers in cool, dark conditions. If it is possible to refrigerate them, that will greatly extend their life.

Vitamin A should have a shelf life of at least two years, if kept sealed at room temperature, and that could be extended to at least five years, if refrigerated. The B vitamins are relatively stable in their dry form, and should be good for three to five years at room temperature. The B vitamins may develop a strong vitamin odor over time, but this in no way indicates that the potency has dropped or the vitamin has gone bad. Vitamin E is similar to vitamin A, that is, a minimum of two years on the shelf, and five years under refrigeration. Vitamin C in powdered form should last a minimum of five years at room temperature, provided it is not opened. The powder may turn slightly yellow with age, but this does not affect the potency. Multiple vitamins should last at least three years if kept sealed and reasonably cool; however, it would be wise to verify the shelf life with the specific manufacturer, since the particular combination of ingredients and the type of manufacturing process affects the shelf life.

Wines

There is no investment quite so appealing as that which yields a dividend of personal pleasure to the investor. For those who enjoy the taste and ritual of wine, the investment in a substantial personal wine cellar offers the best of everything: low risk, protection against inflation, no taxes on the gain, and an interesting and pleasurable avocation—in other words, it is the perfect asset for saving. It is not necessary to have an educated palate, or even an understanding of the difference between a Bordeaux and a Burgundy to profit from an investment in a substantial wine cellar. Connoisseur or not, the dollars saved from advance purchases of wine are a benefit to even the lightest drinker.

Wine has all the benefits of the best savings asset, and a few more. Most of the wines you will consider storing will improve with age; today's $5 Cabernet Sauvignon may become a $50 wine after five more years in the bottle, even without inflation to hurry it along. This benefit is not necessarily one that you can cash in on in dollars and cents, but is a dividend you will collect in pleasure. In this same category falls the benefit of owning and enjoying a wine cellar.

Before buying wine for storage, it's necessary to know which wines store well and which store poorly. This means knowing a little about the basic cultivation and chemistry of wine.

There are five major factors that enter into the quality of a wine before it reaches the bottle: the basic type of grape, the soil in which the grapes were grown, the climate during their growth, the time at which they are picked, and the skill of the vintner in processing the grapes from field to bottle. Once these factors are set and the wine is in the bottle, the future changes in the quality of most wines can be roughly predicted. Some will immediately begin to deteriorate, and some will get better year after year, sometimes taking decades to reach their fullest potential.

Wine changes in the bottle are due to a continuing chemical reaction. The relative abundance or scarcity of certain elements determines the point in time at which the wine will reach its peak of quality. In a young wine, acids, sugars, minerals, pigments, esters, aldehydes, and tannin are all present. These elements are the basic preservatives and their interaction produces the flavor, bouquet, and body of the wine. The more of these elements that are present, the longer it will take the wine to mature, the longer the wine will keep, and the more likely it is that it will be a good or great wine.

Tannin, or tannic acid, is one of the most important preserving and flavoring agents. A young wine high in tannin will mature slowly and enjoy a long life. The red wines of Bordeaux are high in tannin, and thus are generally longer lived than the reds of say, Burgundy, where the reds are higher in glycerine.

Sugars, other acids, and alcohol also act as preservatives. The sweet white Sauternes, with their high sugar content, will keep well, as will those with a high alcohol content such as Port and sweet Sherry. Lighter wines, such as the lighter red Beaujolais and the white Rieslings, are generally lower in some of these critical preserving chemicals, and thus reach maturity rapidly and should be drunk within the first few years after bottling.

In most cases, wine doesn't go bad (in the way that milk goes sour) unless it's exposed to oxygen. When exposed to oxygen, either because of a faulty cork or when opened, the acids turn the wine to vinegar—then the wine is truly spoiled. More often, the wine very gradually loses its body and flavor, and is simply said to be over the hill—not spoiled, but no longer really prime. In general, the better the quality of wine, the later it will mature and the longer it will keep. Bad wines show up early and die young.

Of the European wines, Rheingau, Red Bordeaux, White Burgundy, Chablis, the bigger red Burgundies of the Cote de Nuits, sweet white Sauternes and Chenins of Anjou, red Rhones, and the better Champagnes are good for cellaring. The dry white wines like white Graves, Sauvignon wines of the upper Loire, and Muscadet are not good wines for keeping.

The five most likely candidates for cellaring among the California wines are Cabernet Sauvignon, Zinfandel, Petit Sirah, Sauvignon Blanc, and Pinot Blanc. Chardonnay, California Pinot Noir, and most of the Rieslings are not good keepers.

Wine is a delicate liquid that is constantly undergoing a chemical change. This chemical reaction initially serves to improve the wine, to bring it to maturity, as the tannin in the wine is gradually converted to perfumelike esters. At a certain point, however, the peak of quality is reached, and after that the wine begins to become less pleasurable. Since the speed of a chemical reaction is a factor of the temperature, storing wines at high temperatures will tend to bring them to maturity sooner, and put them over the hill sooner. Lower temperatures will inhibit the chemical process, slowing down both the maturation and extending the ultimate life of the wine. However, it seems to be the consensus that the actual temperature at which the wine is stored is not so critical as keeping the temperature constant. Since underground cellars tend to remain at a more constant temperature, they have been the customary location of the wine. In today's houses, however, real cellars are more and more a thing of the past, so most of us must make other provisions.

Expensive wine racks are not necessary. You can build normal wood shelving into a closet or pantry, and simply store the case of bottles on the shelves. Wine bottles are packed neck-down in their cardboard cartons in order to keep the corks wet. When storing you would be wise to turn the cartons on their sides, thus taking some of the pressure off the corks while still leaving them covered. Don't be paranoid about the storage of your wine. Keep it at a fairly stable temperature and out of direct sunlight, and it will probably keep a reasonable length of time.

How much wealth can you protect? If your family enjoys an average of two bottles of wine per week, you will consume about a thousand bottles in a decade. Stocking 1,000 bottles at an average of $5.00 per bottle would mean a conversion of $5,000 from paper claims into real wealth. If you are a wine lover, this would certainly be one of the very safest and best investments available. You would completely protect the purchasing power of your money, and, assuming you replenish that stock as it's consumed, you would always be drinking wines at prices in effect ten years back, as well as enjoying far better wines than you could hope to buy with the same number of inflated dollars.

Spirits

Wine is not the only alcoholic beverage that can be profitably stockpiled. If you drink scotch, bourbon, vodka, gin, or any of the other hard liquors, you'll find them to be good Alpha items. All should store well for ten years or more, *provided you store them properly*.

First, the bottles must be tightly capped, and it is best not to rely on the bottler to have seen to this. Open the cases and make certain all the bottles are *tightly* sealed. If they have screw-type caps, tighten them. If you're in doubt about the seal, melt some paraffin in a pan, and dip the tops of the bottles in it. If the bottles aren't completely sealed, the alcohol will gradually evaporate, and you'll wind up with lots of solids, and little punch. Second, store them in a dark, cool storage area. Light will cause chemical reactions over long periods that will change the liquor's flavor. Heat, again, will shorten storage life, so keep your cache in a cool environment, preferably below 70 degrees Fahrenheit (the cooler, the better). Finally, do not store your alcoholic beverages around any strong odors. Mothballs, aromatic cedar, gasoline, oil, and all other strong-smelling substances will contaminate them, as the liquor, even though stored in tightly sealed bottles, will absorb these odors.

The flavored liqueurs are not good Alpha items, as their shelf-life is too short. While it varies depending on the type of liqueur, generally a year or two is all that can be counted on before flavors change or are lost.

Beer is definitely out as a way to store your wealth. Its shelf life is estimated at about sixty days. Buy it fresh.

Health & Beauty Aids

Many of the non-drug health and beauty items you commonly buy will keep indefinitely, and most over-the-counter and prescription drugs also have extremely long shelf lives. Even those prescriptions that carry an expiration date will usually retain their potency much longer than is indicated on the package. If you regularly use some medication for a chronic condition, discuss the item with your druggist, and stockpile as much of it as you'll need for the shelf life of the product.

Items such as deodorant, shampoo and toothpaste will keep indefinitely when stored in a cool, dry place, and mouthwash will keep up to three years under these same conditions. Hand creams and face creams will also keep at least two years under cool, dry conditions, and may indeed last longer. While the consumption rates of these items vary substantially from person to person, you can calculate your average annual usage by simply keeping track of how much you use during a month. In the case of toothpaste, the average American brushes away thirty ounces (about three nine-ounce tubes) each year, or about thirty tubes per decade. This means that a family of four can buy ten cases (twelve tubes per case), and thus get inflation protection on another $200 or so of savings.

Although a woman may frequently change her shade or brand of lipstick and nail polish, there are many cosmetic items that remain standard most of her life. Nail polish remover would be an example, as would such things as cold cream and powder. Any of these items would be good Alpha items.

Cosmetics frequently come in small sizes carrying high retail markups, so search for institutional or professional sizes. A beauty supply store will provide some outstanding bargains for the Alpha Strategist.

While reviewing other health and beauty products for stockpiling, don't forget razor blades, toothbrushes, sanitary napkins, combs, brushes, and first-aid supplies. The Appendix lists over fifty common items in this category, but a survey of your bathroom should uncover even more.

Cleaning Supplies

Every family consumes a steady flow of cleaning products, and although most of these things have shelf lives measured in decades, caution is advised, as some things do not. Certain dishwasher detergents, for example, have chemicals added to them that deteriorate rapidly. You may find these detergents on sale and assume that it is a good opportunity to stock up, while in fact the merchant knows that his stock is becoming outdated and he is trying to unload it before it goes bad. Assume that dishwasher detergents have a shelf life of one year, and when buying a year's supply, check the dating code on the box to make certain you are buying fresh merchandise.

The same problem exists in other detergents. Laundry detergent has a problem similar to that of dishwasher detergent. It normally has a shelf life of two years, and after that time it becomes less soluble. The same thing happens with bubble bath. Dishwashing liquid may begin to lose its perfume after two years; however, its cleaning power should not be affected. Fabric softeners, either in sheets or in bottles, will last indefinitely. Again, the perfume will fade after six months or one year, but overall performance will not suffer. Hand soap will keep indefinitely. It may yellow somewhat over the years and you may notice it doesn't lather quite as well, but its cleaning performance will not change.

The best Alpha items in the cleaning equipment category are brushes, brooms, mops, vacuum bags, pot scrubbers, trash bags, compactor bags, sponges, and scouring pads.

With few exceptions, cleaners and cleaning aids offer the Alpha Strategist wide opportunities to protect capital. Again, this is an area where huge initial savings can be made by purchasing the largest institutional sizes. A survey of your kitchen and laundry room will remind you of the items you use most, and for additional suggestions, refer to the list of cleaning items in the Appendix.

Paper Products

Since the use of paper in our lives has been growing rapidly over the past few decades, paper products offer a large area of potential investment. For the most part, paper goods have indefinite shelf lives, providing the paper is not exposed to light or to destruction by insects or mice. The biggest drawback to some of these goods is their low cost per cubic foot, as this makes them costly to store.

Be careful in choosing which paper products to stockpile. "Distributor grades" or "economy grades" contain ground wood, are of a coarser pulp, and tend to yellow with age. "Consumer grades" usually contain no ground wood and so are less susceptible to yellowing. Colored or tinted paper products tend to fade after two years. Facial tissue and toilet tissue will last for years, although paper manufacturers suggest you store them for no longer than five years. Manufacturers do not indicate a specific length of time for storing paper towels and napkins, but since they contain "wet strength resins," they lose their softness, their absorptive qualities, and become brittle in a few years.

Among the most sensible items to stockpile are the things you consume in the greatest quantities. This would usually include paper towels, toilet paper, wax paper, plastic wrap, aluminum foil, paper plates and cups, notebook paper, gift wrap, and perhaps disposable diapers.

Clothing & Softgoods

When considering clothing, the primary question is one of fashion. Stockpile only those things that you know you will not object to wearing five, ten, or twenty years from now, no matter how styles may change in the meantime. At first glance, it might seem that there would be little in this category that wouldn't go out of style, but on closer examination you will probably find a great many items that you regularly wear which never change.

The average man should be able to stockpile a ten- or twenty-year supply of socks, underwear, work pants and shirts, t-shirts, handkerchiefs, sweaters, and pajamas, as well as protective gear such as raincoats, overcoats, and umbrellas. Even though a man may not want to buy a twenty-year supply of shoes, it still makes sense to buy three or four pairs at a time, especially if he tends to buy the same styles.

Every woman could stockpile pantyhose, bras, slips, socks, nightgowns, robes, as well as housedresses, slippers, and sweaters.

In addition to clothing, there are many areas of the home where fabrics are used. Softgoods represent one of the best areas for storing value. Consider stockpiling at least a twenty-year supply of face towels, bath towels, dish towels, sheets, pillow cases, pillows, blankets, and bedspreads.

Automobiles, Gasoline, and Accessories

Storage space and styling taken into account, you may decide to buy an extra new car this year and put it up on blocks. Five years from now, you might find yourself very pleased with your foresight, both from the standpoint of the price increases you avoided and from the quality changes that occur. In many products, particularly automobiles, the new models do not always represent improvements on the old ones. Not only does inflation tempt the manufacturers to reduce quality instead of increasing prices, government safety and pollution requirements seem to force the auto makers to produce lower powered, higher maintenance-cost cars each year.

When you buy a new car, stock up on all the replacement parts that you are likely to need over the life of the vehicle. This would include extra fan belts, radiator hoses, spark plugs, ignition sets, air filters, oil filters, batteries, brake shoes, and tires. The batteries will be stored dry. Since battery acid might be dangerous to store, and is relatively inexpensive anyway, it could be purchased when you are ready to activate the battery. All of these parts have indefinite shelf lives, and will do nothing but go up in value. If you drive a hard bargain with the salesman when you buy the car, he may provide the parts at dealer cost.

When buying tires and batteries in advance, you must arrange for the guarantees to be initiated when these parts are actually installed on the car. If you promise to let the dealer be the one to install them, he will probably agree.

The gasoline shortage has made many people consider storing gasoline. This would appear to be a very smart move but there are drawbacks. First, gasoline manufacturers point out that gasoline does not store well. Chemicals in the fuel break down, and the maximum storage life is only about one year. After that it still burns, but it does not have the octane rating the modern high-performance engine requires.

The second problem is storage. You need the room and the equipment to put it away. Assuming you have two cars, drive about 15,000 miles per year in each vehicle, and average 15 miles per gallon, you will use 2,000 gallons per year. A 2,000-gallon tank will cost you approximately $4,000 to install, complete with pump. In most areas, you'll need a building permit from your local bureaucrat, as well as permission from the fire department. The tank companies that service your area will be able to determine whether the acidity of your soil requires any special coatings on the tank.

If you do decide to install a tank, get through the tangle of bureaucratic red tape, and get it functioning, you can expect to save about 10 percent on your gasoline costs by buying in large quantities, plus having the inflation protection on the gasoline between the time you buy it and the time you use it, which, if you buy a year's supply, should average about six months. The dollar savings may be a small benefit compared to the convenience of avoiding the lines at the gas stations.

Do not assume that you will completely avoid shortages if the energy situation deteriorates. You will be required to let the Department of Energy know about your tank, and they will determine how big a gasoline allocation you can have. If rationing is instituted, you can bet they will be out to check on just how much gas you have stored away, and they will see to it that you do not benefit from your foresight.

Motor oil is another auto product that you should consider storing. Again, the oil companies claim that the detergent oils have a shelf life of about two years. Nondetergent oils, such as Quaker State, and Pennzoil have indefinite shelf lives. If you drive 15,000 miles per year per car, you should use about ten to fifteen quarts per year per car. A two-year supply of detergent oil would therefore be about thirty quarts, while if you use nondetergent, you could stockpile up to 200 quarts per car. You can save some money by buying the oil in gallon containers.

Don't forget to stockpile anti-freeze, brake fluid, transmission fluid, and all the polishes and waxes you'll be using.

Miscellaneous Alpha Items

Besides the standard categories of goods above, there are many interests individuals have that offer opportunities for investing substantial sums.

Sports, recreation, and hobbies are fertile areas in which to find stockpiling opportunities. Whether it is exercise equipment and clothes, camping gear, photographic supplies, golf balls, or woodworking equipment, each person's particular interests should be explored and integrated into the Alpha Stragegy.

Don't forget that you can stockpile gifts to be given away in the future. Think forward to birthdays, anniversaries, graduations, and religious holidays. With a little forethought, you'll probably find that you can buy your gifts at least a year or two in advance, if not longer. It will save you a lot of shopping time, relieve holiday pressure, and beat inflation to boot.

Sources of Supply

Once you've embarked on Level Two of the Alpha Strategy, and you've selected the items and quantities that are appropriate, you'll be ready to locate sources of supply. You'll find a variety of different distributors for products, including retail stores, discount stores, cooperatives, catalog suppliers, wholesalers, jobbers, industrial suppliers, and the manufacturers themselves. Which you use will depend on the quantity of the item you use, whether you insist on a brand name, and the proximity of the source.

The large supermarket chains are a reasonable source for bulk purchases of food and drug items. They buy in huge quantities at maximum discounts, and operate on narrow profit margins. While most of them will not offer case discounts, their prices are so low on some items that you won't need them.

The grocery business is extremely competitive, and grocers learned long ago that they could attract shoppers into their stores by advertising special prices on common items. A market will frequently offer loss leaders at below cost in order to bring you into the store. Since the grocer may be selling below his cost on some staple, he might limit the quantity to each customer. Don't expect the grocer to thank you for buying ten cases of some product that he's letting go at cost. He's had to buy the stuff, move it around, and deliver it to you, at no profit. Your best bet, in order to retain his good will, is to tell him what you're doing and offer to pay him a

Table I

ITEM	National Retail Dept. Store	Super Market	Member- ship Discount	Drug Chain	Whlsl	Price Variation
Anti-freeze						
Prestone, 1 gal.	$4.29	$4.69	$3.37	$3.99	n/a	39%
Lightbulbs						
G.E., standard	.44	.74	.54	.77	n/a	75%
Trash bags (8)						
Glad, hvwt, 3-mil	n/a	1.92	1.43	2.29	1.99	60%
Shampoo						
Johnson's Baby, 16 oz.	2.42	2.85	2.19	3.19	2.64	46%
Toothpaste						
Crest, 7 oz.	1.32	1.35	1.09	1.39	1.20	27%
Hand soap						
Camay, bath size	n/a	.43	.41	.45	.37	10%
Toothbrushes						
Oral B, adult 40	1.19	.99	.75	1.09	.61	59%
Mouthwash						
Scope, 18 oz.	1.71	1.69	1.26	1.71	1.38	36%
Petroleum jelly						
Vaseline, 15 oz.	1.69	1.81	1.22	1.90	1.44	56%
Facial tissue						
Kleenex, 200 reg.	.75	.74	.59	.75	.62	27%
Aluminum foil						
Reynolds, 200 sq. ft.	n/a	2.96	2.43	2.99	2.59	23%
Tampons						
Tampax, 40 tampons	2.33	2.09	1.77	2.19	1.70	32%
					Average variation	41%

handling fee for any items he's selling to you at cost.

A few discount department stores also handle food items and should be checked for price comparisons. In our area, the lowest prices for regular household items are found at a local membership discount store. It consistently beats even the largest supermarket chains for most items, and in some cases sells for well below what those markets must pay for the same items.

A couple of places that appear to be inexpensive, but which actually are often higher than supermarkets on nonfood drug and grocery items, are the discount drug chains, cash and carry wholesale grocers, and national retail department stores. As an Alpha Strategist you will have to check different sources in your area for the best prices on each item. Just to help you recognize how profitable this might be. In Table I I've listed price comparisons on a dozen Alpha items priced at different types of retailers in the Los Angeles area.

You'll notice I've included the wholesale price of most items, and you'll find that some items can be purchased at prices below wholesale. This can happen for a number of reasons. Some retailers may make direct purchases from manufacturers, thus bypassing the wholesaler. Some may sell certain items at a loss to attract customers. There are often special deals made by wholesalers and manufacturers on certain items. In any case, you can see from the following price comparisons that there are great opportunities for savings just by doing a little shopping. Incidentally, these price comparisons were made in early 1980, and all in the Southern California area. They aren't intended to indicate what you would be able to buy these things for in your area at the time you read this.

Take one of the items from my list with the lowest percentage differential between retailers—toothpaste is an example. If your family uses twelve tubes per year, you'll use about 120 tubes in the next decade. Since the price variation is around 25 percent on toothpaste and a tube sells for a high of $1.38, your potential saving is thirty cents per tube, or $36.00 for checking just that one price! Since you should be able to check prices of at least fifty items in one day's effort, you could earn as much as $1,000 or more for that one day's work.

Brand Name Versus Private Label

Private label merchandise is not a new phenomenon. Sears, Safeway and many other retailers have always had their own brands of merchandise. Although these products are often manufactured by the same companies that put out the nationally advertised brands, and frequently are identical to those brands, the prices are usually lower. The major reason private label articles are cheaper is that they do not carry the enormous advertising costs which weigh down the brand name goods. When a manufacturer is calculating the margin of profit on his main line, he adds in advertising, marketing, and special promotion costs, as well as his actual production and overhead costs. If a retail chain places an order for private-label products, the manufacturer excludes marketing and promotion costs when arriving at a price. The business is good for the manufacturer, as it pays him a profit and keeps his manufacturing facility operating at higher production levels, thus amortizing his fixed overhead over more units of production. It is good for the retailer, because it allows him to offer his own brand at a lower cost than the national brand, and thus attracts more cost-conscious customers. It's good for the customer, because it offers him lower prices.

When you are planning your Alpha portfolio, compare the quality and cost of some of the private label brands against the national brands you've been using. You may be pleasantly surprised.

Larger Containers Mean Savings

Everyone realizes that smaller containers result in a higher cost per unit of volume. In this day of mass production and fancy packaging, the package itself is often the major cost. Always buy the largest size you can conveniently use; if this turns out to be the industrial or institutional size, your savings can really add up.

In the case of canned goods, restaurants will usually buy things like canned fruit, olives, condiments, spices, etc., in gallon or five-gallon jars or cans. As a single consumer you can't normally take advantage of these larger containers, since you don't consume that much of one item at one sitting. A number ten can of peaches, for example, contains six pounds of fruit. It sells at about 20 percent less per pound than the smaller can, but the average consumer would probably throw at least 20 percent of the larger can away. An alternative would be to buy the large size, open the can, and freeze what you don't use in small containers, so you can use it a bit at a time.

Professional beauty supply stores offer excellent values for Alpha Strategists. Take shampoo, for example. A local beauty supply store offered a one-gallon jug of Breck shampoo for $8.95 (less 10 percent to regular customers). At the same time, local drug and grocery stores were selling 16-ounce bottles for $2.50, which is the equivalent of $20.00 per gallon. Since a family of four can go through as much as two gallons per year, buying a ten-year supply at a beauty supply store would save a family about $250, in addition to the inflation protection gained by stockpiling. Putting this in an investment perspective, an equivalent investment would have to be risk-free yet provide you with a tax-free, fully inflation-adjusted cash flow of 25 percent per year. How can you lose?

The moral is, buy the large institutional sizes whenever you can. Get your beauty supplies from a beauty supply shop, your cleaning fluids and soaps from a laundry supply outlet, and your staple food items from a restaurant supply store.

A note of caution. *Always check prices.* Never assume that an item is competitively priced merely because the sign over the door says "wholesale." In the "cash and carry" wholesale outlets which cater to small grocery stores and restaurants, the regular consumer sizes may be just as expensive as they are in the large supermarket chains. In some cases, even the institutional sizes are more expensive. It pays to compare.

Storage

Once you've decided to become an Alpha Strategist, you'll need to think about the storage problem. The amount of room you need will depend on the amount of money you have to invest, and the type of goods you decide to stockpile. Since goods usually come packed in cardboard boxes of specific dimensions, it's possible to develop a rough estimate of storage requirements by figuring out the average cost per cubic foot of the goods you'll be buying, and dividing that figure into the total amount of money you intend to invest in goods.

To give you an idea of how much space cases of Alpha items might take up relative to the cost of those items, Table II offers

Table II

Item	Value per Cubic Foot
Viva paper towels	$ 4.10
Purina dog chow	6.10
Northern toilet tissue	6.20
Kleenex	10.50
Comet cleanser	12.20
Joy dishwashing liquid	15.30
Wheat	17.20
Cascade dishwasher detergent	27.60
Tires (HR-70/15 steel radial)	28.10
G.E. lightbulbs	30.50
Camay bath soap	61.00
Smirnoff vodka	112.70
Aluminum foil (12" x 1,000')	123.00
Gillette Trac II razor blades	845.00

some examples. The value per cubic foot figures were calculated by dividing the item's average retail price by the carton's volume.

Assuming that the average value per cubic foot of goods you'll be storing is $25.00, then a $10,000 stockpile will require 400 cubic feet of space. It could be kept in a space four-feet deep by seven-feet high by fourteen-feet long, or roughly a four-foot deep storage area built along the wall of your garage.

There are a number of considerations as to where and how you store your goods. High temperatures, humidity, and light are the principal enemies of any type of goods. Most deterioration comes from chemical changes, and most chemical reactions increase as temperatures increase. In addition, certain rays present in light cause chemical changes. Light fades many dyes and causes other forms of physical deterioration. Humidity can increase oxidation, can cause molecules to bond together (as when sugar and salt cake up), and can provide an environment conducive to the reproduction of fungus, insects, and other destructive pests.

The ideal storage system will minimize deterioration by providing a cool, dark and dry environment for your goods. The storage area should be arranged so that cartons are not stacked directly on cement floors or against cement or brick walls, since moisture will seep through. If convenient, the storage area can be completely lined with inexpensive plastic sheeting to ensure it will be moistureproof. The area should be free of cracks and holes to prevent insect and rodent entrance, and insect repellents and poisons (moth balls, ant powders, etc.) should be placed in the area to take care of any organisms that do get inside. Remember, however, that you shouldn't put any aromatic substances in areas where you'll be storing liquors.

Since light is an enemy to your goods, avoid the temptation to store them on open shelves and take the trouble to install some type of cover such as sliding panels or doors. For goods particularly vulnerable to moisture, you may want to seal the individual cartons with wax, plastic, or some other waterproof material prior to storing them.

Besides protecting the goods from deterioration, you're also concerned about pilferage from neighborhood children and loss to burglars. The best protection in this regard is to avoid broadcasting the fact that you have a substantial stockpile, and to make certain the storage area is securely locked. You can also consider camouflaging your storage area in hopes that intruders won't be aware of its existence. This could be done by constructing a false wall, a hidden door in a closet, or the like. It would be inexpensive and easy to install a burglar alarm that would scare the burglar away and alert you or your neighbors to a break-in.

There are a number of areas in the home that can be considered for your cache. If your home has a basement, it could be the very best location, provided you don't anticipate any type of flooding. Basements tend to stay cooler all year long, are less vulnerable to break-in, and are out of the way. The main drawback will probably be moisture. You'll need to raise your goods off the damp cement floor, and seal the walls thoroughly to prevent damage.

Attics are another potential storage area, as are the crawl spaces between the ceilings and roofs of most single-story houses. The major drawback to these areas is temperature, so only those goods not affected by temperature should be stored there. This is the ideal area to store those goods affected by moisture, since these spaces are usually dry.

A good idea for that crawl space above the ceiling is to install two 2 x 4-inch "tracks" the length of the area, and build simple platforms on rollers to ride the tracks. You can load your goods onto the platforms and then run them back and forth on the tracks with ropes. This method will eliminate your need to crawl around in that cramped area when you want to store or retrieve your goods.

The garage is an obvious storage area, but it has its drawbacks. First, it is usually easily broken into, and very convenient for the thief, since he can back his truck right up to your goods. The garage is often poorly insulated, so heat and moisture may be more of a problem.

Many other spots can be found in the average home, and unless a very large stockpile is held, a little careful organization of your present belongings can result in room for a fairly large cache right in the nooks and crannies of the main living areas. Cases and individual items can be stored in closets, under counters, under beds, under tables, and in unused bedrooms.

Once the possibilities for storage in the home have been exhausted, and you still have goods to store, there are many options still open. You may have a relative or close friend who has substantial spare storage space he would give or rent to you; you can rent space at a commercial warehouse or in one of the new mini-storage units; and, in some cases, you may be able to leave the merchandise with the merchant from whom you've purchased it by paying him a small storage charge.

Survey your home and decide what is available without construction or remodeling, make rough estimates of what any storage space construction might cost, and finally compare this cost with the cost of renting separate storage facilities.

While the costs of outside facilities will vary from place to place, at early 1981 price levels, you should be able to rent space for no more than $3.50 per square foot per year. Assuming you could stack your goods seven feet high, the storage cost is fifty cents per cubic foot per year. Thus, if your goods are valued at an average of $25.00 per cubic foot, you will be paying about 2 percent of value per year for storage. An analysis of the cost of storage will soon convince you that the most practical Alpha items are those with the highest value per cubic foot.

Insurance

The risk of losing your investment values through theft, fire, or any other natural disaster is something you may want to cover through insurance.

When should you insure? Whenever losing the goods would cause you an economic loss which would affect your standard of living in any significant way. For example, if your total investment assets are $10,000, losing them would mean a significant reduction in your standard of living, either now or when the point comes at which you would be consuming those goods. Since the loss is significant to you, you should cover it with insurance. If you have a net worth of $250,000, however, and have $10,000 in Alpha Strategy goods stored at home, their loss would probably not affect your standard of living. In this case, you would not insure.

This concept of insuring only when a loss would affect your standard of living is derived from the fact that insurance companies charge rates higher than the statistical probability of a loss, and thus they profit. By acting as your own insurance company in those cases where you are financially able to absorb the loss, you stand to earn that profit.

Whether you insure with an outside company, or insure by taking the risk yourself, recognize that there is a cost involved. The cost of insurance will depend upon your location (fire rates, for example, are determined by the probability of fires in different areas), and the amount of goods you'll be covering. If you own your home and carry homeowner's insurance, you probably have coverage on the contents of your home. Most homeowner's policies cover contents to 50 percent of the coverage carried on the structure itself; thus, if you carry $100,000 on the structure, you could receive as high as $50,000 on the contents in the event of a loss. If your Alpha items raise the total value of the contents of your home above the content limits of your homeowner's policy, you'll need to add coverage. If you're a tenant, you can purchase a renter's policy that covers your belongings, but not the structure of the building. Again, the cost will vary by area.

Most policies cover just about any type of loss except earthquake and flood losses. If you want insurance against these losses, you'll need special endorsements, or separate policies. Earthquake insurance will probably run $2.00 per $1,000 of value, or less. Flood insurance is available only through the federal government.

Although costs of homeowners' and tenants' policies vary from company to company and from area to area, you can assume that insurance on your cache of goods will cost somewhere around $5.00 per $1,000 of value per year. This means that you'll be spending about one-half of one percent of the value of the goods each year for insurance. It's inexpensive, but remember, don't buy it unless you really need it.

If you decide to store your Alpha items in a mini-warehouse, or in some other place off your premises, you'll need a separate policy. This type of policy is a bit more expensive than a tenant's or homeowner's policy, and will probably cost you about $12.00 per $1,000 per year, or about 1.2 percent of the value of the goods annually.

When insured, you should be prepared to make a claim that will not be turned down by the insurance company. The thing the insurer wants is reasonable proof of loss. In order to verify a loss, you'll need evidence that the goods really did exist. (This will hold true whether you're dealing with an insurance company, or trying to substantiate a casualty deduction on your tax return.) The Alpha Strategist should keep an inventory of the goods in his stockpile, and should also keep all receipts for those goods so that their value can be verified. Since stockpiling is a rather unusual pursuit, I would suggest you invite your insurance agent to your house and show him what you're doing. Explain your inventory system, and ask him how he would suggest you prepare yourself for the possibility of a loss.

When discussing the problem with your agent, make it clear that you want insurance on the *replacement* value of the goods, not on their cost. If you've had the goods for some time, those goods will have increased in value significantly, and you don't want to be stuck with insurance that only gives you back what you originally paid (or less).

Conclusion

Everyone should have a personal savings account of consumables, whether he has $500 of investment capital or $5 million. It is not just a system for protecting investment dollars against the ravages of inflation, taxation, and market risk. It is a time-saving, convenient, and rational method of living.

The goods you buy and stockpile will be unique to you, and will fit your own particular situation. The items mentioned above are meant only to stimulate your thinking and offer a few general guidelines. You'll no doubt discover many other things you can store away, while rejecting many of the things I have mentioned. Just keep in mind that the most important items are those with the highest value per cubic foot. You might also think about the potential scarcity of certain items in the future, and make certain those items are included in your portfolio. Remember, however, that the idea behind the Alpha Strategy is not to prepare for shortages or disaster, but merely to protect dollars against inflation.

CHAPTER TEN

_____

LEVEL THREE:
SAVE REAL MONEY

For the last 200 pages we have walked a zig-zag path through the carnival of the great American economy. After a brief introduction to the nature and source of wealth, and with a few fundamental economic laws to help you understand how the games are played, I exposed the sting. You saw how the players are fleeced (usually with their own consent and assistance) and how the theft is camouflaged under the cloak of law. We toured the conventional savings and investment markets, and uncovered numerous traps and pitfalls that await the individual who would try to store his wealth there. Finally, we concluded that the swindle of inflation, the theft of taxation and regulation, and the false premises of the investment markets left only one safe way to preserve wealth for the future: the Alpha Strategy.

In Chapter Eight, I argued that the first level of your savings should be directed toward accumulating knowledge and the tools of production in order to increase and secure your income. The second level of the strategy, detailed in Chapter Nine, is to invest the maximum possible in those goods that you can buy now, store, and eventually consume. Now you must take stock of your remaining wealth. If you have significant paper claims left, you are ready to explore the third level of the strategy: the accumulation of real goods that you can eventually sell or exchange. By the dictates of reason and common sense, we are forced to return to the beginning—commodity money.

Exchangeable real goods fall into three basic categories: (1) manufactured goods, (2) collectibles, and (3) raw commodities.

Manufactured Goods

The production and consumption goods stockpiled for your home and business are all manufactured goods. When stored for personal use, they represent a near-perfect method of preserving the value of your wealth. There is a major difference, however, between buying these items for consumption and stockpiling them for eventual sale.

The problem lies in marketing, as sales and marketing expenses normally comprise the majority of the retail price of any product. Stockpiling these goods for eventual sale means that at the other end you will face marketing costs, costs that will be higher for you than for the original seller, since you're probably not in that business. Since these costs may run 50 percent or more of the item's retail value, the financial benefits of this portion of the Alpha Strategy would be significantly diminished, if not destroyed.

A second problem with stockpiling manufactured goods is change. Manufacturers engage in a constant battle for markets, and this competition drives them to continually modify and improve their products. New models, new improvements, and new package designs flood the market, all vying for the attention of consumers. The Alpha Strategist who tries to resell his cache will find a serious competitive disadvantage in entering the marketplace with ten- or twenty-year-old goods, even though the only change may be the label design.

Manufactured products are poor choices as mediums of exchange.

Collectibles

The second type of real goods that might be considered are collectibles, including such things as antiques, rare coins, stamps, Chinese ceramics, rare books, autographs of famous people, and commemoratives.

Anyone who reads newspapers is aware of the incredible prices paid for scarce collectibles. A 1918 "inverted" airmail stamp sold recently for $72,500; an 1879 $4 gold piece for over $100,000; a set of eighteenth century Chippendale chairs for over $200,000. The price boom in collectibles has been responsible for attracting tens of thousands of investors and speculators into this market, and many people feel that these things offer the best possible protection for wealth. Do they?

Most collectibles have one thing in common: their *utility value*, that is, the portion of their value attributable to the useful purpose they serve, is a minute fraction of their total exchange value. Whether it's a painting, a diamond, a rare coin, or an antique chair, the demand is a result of the rarity or beauty of the object, not its utility.

There are two types of buyers for collectibles: collectors who hold them for the pleasure they receive, and investors or speculators who hold them for profit. Collector interest comes first. Investors are attracted only after a wide collector market has been established and prices have begun to rise. Inflation adds to the scenario. If an increasing quantity of money, in addition to a growing number of collectors, meets with a fixed supply of some collectible, the price of that item rises more rapidly, and investors are even more likely to notice. Simultaneously, inflation will cause savers and investors to look around for alternatives to depreciating savings accounts and bond investments.

These factors have caused the boom in collectibles over the past decade. If inflation accelerates, many collectibles may enjoy further gains, but the gains will not be due to an increase in the usefulness of these things relative to other goods. It will be the result of the growing fever that drives speculators toward any assets that have been rising in price more rapidly than average. It is this weak foundation for value that makes collectibles dangerous. Any drop in demand that causes a particular collectible to fall in price may precipitate an exodus by investors and speculators that can lead to a total price collapse.

History is replete with examples of speculative excess and eventual price collapse, but perhaps the most famous is the tulip mania that swept Holland in the seventeenth century. Tulips were introduced to the country in 1600. Their beauty gradually created a following of collectors, and prices began to rise. Within thirty years after their introduction, a speculative market developed that became so large the bulbs were eventually traded on the stock exchange. In his famous book, *Extraordinary Popular Delusions and the Madness of Crowds*, Charles MacKay described the folly:

> As the mania increased, prices augmented, until, in the year 1636, many persons were known to invest a fortune of 100,000 florins in the purchase of forty roots . . . At first, as in all these gambling mania, confidence was at its height, and everybody gained. The tulip-jobbers speculated by buying when prices fell, and selling out when they rose. Many individuals grew suddenly rich. A golden bait hung temptingly out before the people, and one after the other they rushed to the tulip-marts, like flies around the honey-pot. Everyone imagined that the passion for tulips would last forever.

But it didn't. The bubble burst, and by the end of 1636, bulbs that had sold for 6,000 florins apiece had fallen to 500. Within a few years, prices fell back to a few florins per bulb.

You could easily read stamps, Chinese porcelain, or almost any other modern day collectible into that story in place of tulip bulbs, and the numbers and sequence would fit perfectly. Remember, the seventeenth century brokers who dealt in those bulbs sold them on their performance record, just as the brokers of today use the price history of the past two or three decades to sell the collectibles currently in fashion.

Collectibles are not a sure-fire inflation hedge. They move higher when inflation accelerates, but at the later stages of monetary turmoil they prove fickle and dangerous. Their price appreciation depends solely on the investor's hope that the next investor in the chain will pay a higher price than the investor before him. But the only reason the next person will pay more is because he, in turn, believes the person after him will pay even more. All this while, the usefulness of the collectible remains unchanged. For awhile, prices do appreciate, but with each price increase, the gap between the intrinsic value and the market price widens. As is the case in every pyramid scheme, eventually someone is left holding the bag.

Collectibles are real goods, but they are not consumable goods, and thus, for the average saver and investor they should be approached with extreme caution. You may buy some rare object today and triple or quadruple your money over the next two or three years, but the potential for large gains is not a sound argument for gambling.

A hard look at economic fundamentals will convince you that the best and safest investments in the long run are those that are tied to real, tangible wealth, and whose values do not rest solely on the shifting sand of investor psychology. The only underlying value to collectibles is the pleasure they provide collectors. Once a collectible becomes the object of speculation, the price increases are solely due to a belief in further price increases. Speculative fever makes a poor shelter for your wealth.

Raw Commodities

This brings us to the third and final possibility: using raw commodities as real money. Raw commodities are those real goods that are traded on the producer level, and which are either marketed to wholesalers and retailers for eventual sale to the public, or are used as the raw materials in the production of finished goods. They may be agricultural products, or minerals and chemicals we mine or pump from the ground. They include grains, animal products like pork bellies, eggs, and hides, fruits, lumber, sugar, rubber, oil, raw chemicals, and metals such as copper, zinc, gold, lead, tin, and silver.

These raw commodities have one major characteristic in common: they never go out of style. They are always in demand, and the markets for them are large; consequently, they are relatively simple to resell at any time. They are also used worldwide. This means you can buy and store them in any area of the world and be assured a waiting market when it's time to sell.

Because they are normally sold in large quantities, raw commodities carry a relatively small markup from producer to buyer. This is a major advantage to the stockpiler, buffering him from the high reselling costs that make manufactured goods prohibitive as an investment.

Finally, the quality or purity of raw commodities is easy to determine, which is necessary for convenience in trade.

Perhaps you noticed that the attributes I'm describing are similar to the attributes discussed earlier relative to things that make a good *money*. You're right. Money always originates as a commodity of some kind, and thus commodities are, in essence, money. To find the best commodities for Level Three, simply look for the commodities that meet the qualifications of a good money.

The Gold/Silver Standard

As societies develop, they build strength on the soundness of their money. As the more clever con men learn to plunder savers through government debasement of the currency, saving becomes futile, investment markets succumb to the fever of speculation, and the society gradually crumbles. During this sequence, individuals do their best to protect their wealth, eventually fleeing from paper money, while the plunderers try to use the guns of government to block all exits from the field of slaughter. Law after law is passed to prevent the person with wealth from protecting it. Legal tender laws, laws that confiscate or control gold and silver, price controls, and foreign exchange controls are all examples of this attempt to prevent the citizen from avoiding the consequences of depreciating money.

The average investor or saver is eventually destroyed by inflation, because, in his desperate search for a safe haven for his wealth, he fails to see the obvious. If his plight resulted from the debasement of the medium of exchange, his answer must lie in a return to another strong medium with all the characteristics that made the original medium sound. Instead, he is drawn into pursuit of the illusory profits that seem to be offered by the gyrating investment markets.

You might conclude from this train of thought that I'm suggesting people privately revert back to bartering gold and silver again. However, when one or even two metals serve the function of money in society, they become vulnerable to political control. Indeed, this is just what happened in the past: the government first established the acceptance of its currency by backing it with gold and silver; it then passed legal tender laws to force acceptance of this gold- or silver-backed currency; and, finally, it removed the collateral from behind the paper. It was done so gradually that the people hardly noticed, but eventually inflation resulted and the people naturally began to abandon the currency. To prevent this, the government took control of both of these monetary metals, and, through a series of laws (which included calling in the gold, outlawing its ownership, fixing its price, and manipulating the silver price), it managed to slow the public's escape.

When the government has only two metals to fight, it can easily bring the guns of law to bear. If the use of gold and silver as a private medium of exchange becomes widespread among the public, the government might use the force of law again to inhibit the public's ability to successfully trade in these metals and thus this avenue could be blocked.

The second impediment to a private gold and silver barter system in competition with a depreciating currency is that the uncertainty of the future inflation rate causes the precious metals to undergo violent price gyrations. For money to be a sound medium of exchange, people must be able to count on the stability of its purchasing power. As confidence in the future value of paper currency fluctuates with each month's figures on inflation, industrial production, and news of international conflict, investors and speculators move in and out of gold and silver, causing violent price swings. When people feel secure about the future value of gold and silver, those things can be used as a medium of exchange; but otherwise, they cannot.

If individuals cannot privately reinstitute gold and silver as a barter medium, perhaps the answer to our economic dilemma rests on a *legal* return to the gold standard. If Congress would abandon the credit-backed money, and back currency with gold again, the gold price would stabilize, money creation would stop, and inflation would disappear.

Unfortunately, solving our economic problems is not a simple matter of passing a law to reestablish gold or any other commodity as money. It was not the politicians, but rather *the electorate* that demanded the abandonment of the gold standard and the establishment of a credit-money standard. In a nation run by majority rule, unless you can convince individuals to abandon the use of government as a sword of theft, gold or any other commodity will never last as the basis for money. A gold standard is not the *cause* of a stable economy, it is the *result* of a stable economy; it is not the solution to our problem, but will be one of the consequences when a solution is found. We had a gold standard in the U.S. for over 150 years, yet it didn't prevent our current economic debacle. Establish it again, and it will be abandoned again. In fact, it may be established again just as a sly trick to restore confidence in the value of currency, since backing the dollar with gold would make people think that our problems were solved. But the problems will not be solved, not until the use of government as a method of plunder is stopped.

As an individual, you don't need to waste your time dreaming about the day a gold standard will be reinstituted; you don't need to struggle with the problems of bartering gold or silver; nor do you need to deal in any medium of exchange that is likely to be attacked by government. You can personally establish your own private hard-money economy right now—you can abandon paper and place your wealth in real, raw commodities.

Selection Criteria

Let's distill from all the choices the most practical commodities to hold. First, you want commodities that will not deteriorate over long holding periods, and this eliminates most of the food commodities. Pork bellies, eggs, chickens, potatoes, etc., are out.

Second, you want commodities that are likely to remain reasonably stable in value. Since supply is a component of value, if the production (and thus supply) of a commodity can be drastically increased through technological breakthroughs, the commodity would be less attractive as a store of value.

Third, you want commodities that are reasonably easy to store and transport, and that have a high value per unit of volume or weight, so that your storage and handling costs become a low percentage of your investment. This is another strike against food commodities, since they are bulky and require special storage conditions.

All the criteria for a good long-term store-of-value item point once again to the same commodities that have always been the ultimate choice for money throughout history: the metals. Metals are durable, easily recognized, can be divided into small lots for trade, and are easy to transport and store. They are also scarce in nature, which inhibits the rapid expansion of production, and thus stabilizes their values. I believe that at this point in our economic cycle, industrial metals are the great, overlooked inflation hedge.

Precious Metals

Inflation and international tension cause individuals to search for assets that can be hidden away, and gold and silver are the most widely accepted assets in this category; consequently, prices will rise and fall like a barometer of political turmoil. Price volatility should not preclude these metals from being considered as long term holdings, but it makes them less attractive.

For individuals with substantial wealth, gold and silver should constitute a *portion* of your metals portfolio, but certainly not all. When purchased for the long term, price fluctuations can be ignored, and the investor can be reasonably confident that both metals will act as hedges against any serious deterioration of the world economic or political situation. For the person with modest wealth, a small cache of common gold or silver coins can act as an insurance policy against disruptions in the monetary system. It seems to me, however, that with the substantial risk of government intervention in these markets, and with the certainty of volatile price action, gold and silver no longer offer the stability necessary for the majority of the wealth of the average investor. Fortunately, there are other choices.

The Industrial and Strategic Metals

There are a number of common metals used in industry that fit most of our criteria quite nicely. Copper, zinc, lead, tin, nickel, and aluminum are all metals that can be stockpiled, are universally used, and can be expected to be in demand for centuries to come. While their values will fluctuate, these fluctuations will probably fall within a narrow range. As an example of this stability of value that these metals might provide, look at copper. Historically, a loaf of bread and a pound of copper have maintained their value relative to one another for decades—you could always buy roughly one loaf of bread with one pound of copper. It is likely that this relationship will continue, with minor short-term fluctuations, for many decades, if not centuries, to come. Many other metals will probably enjoy the same price stability. There are at least thirty other metals that could be stockpiled, such as mercury, platinum, palladium, chromium, cobalt, cadmium, and tungsten.

The wisest plan is to diversify in order to hedge against the risk that any single metal will fall in value for an extended length of time, or be adversely affected by government controls. For example, savings of copper, zinc, and lead would offer the Alpha Strategist both inflation protection, and protection against isolated economic problems that might affect individual metals. The best protection would be to diversify into six or eight of the metals.

When to Buy

Over the long term, the selling price of any common product is directly related to the cost of production. Producers will not produce unless they can make a profit. If the profit available from producing one product is substantially greater than the profits available from producing other things, the higher-profit product will attract an influx of entrepreneurs and capital. Production will thus increase, and the increased supply will drive prices down. Profit acts like an automatic governor on an engine: higher profits accelerate production until greater supply reduces prices and thus profits. Lower profits slow production until lower supply creates higher prices, and thus higher profits. We can deduce, therefore, that the price of any common product, including the industrial metals, will tend, *over the long term*, to equal the costs of production plus a reasonable profit to the producer.

Of course, the cost of production can change. When products are first brought into the market, the cost of production is high, as the technology of production is in its infancy, resulting in a high end-product price, and a relatively narrow market. As improving technology causes a drop in production costs, the product's price falls, and the market expands. Expanding production results in economies of scale that cause production costs to fall even further. Opposing this drop is inflation, which pushes costs in the opposite direction. As the value of money falls, costs of production rise, and so the cost of the end product also rises.

While production costs of metal are the long-term determinants of price, over the short term the price of a product is affected by other things. The demand for a metal will fluctuate with the economy, and with changing tastes and technology. In a recession, for example, the demand for goods tends to fall—e.g., people buy fewer automobiles, and automobile manufacturers buy less steel, aluminum, copper, and chromium. Likewise, when the technological breakthroughs cause industry to shift from one material to another, demand changes—e.g., copper wire may suffer from falling demand as fiber optics become more widely used in the transmission of telephone signals. If demand for a product falls due to recession, it is likely to pick up again once the recession is over. However, if it falls due to changing technology, the decline in production may be permanent.

Whether declining demand is permanent or temporary, however, the price decline accompanying it is almost always short-lived. The initial price decline is caused by the amount of the metal held in the inventories of the producers and consumers, as well as the relatively high production levels of the producing companies. Inventory and production levels stabilize at a given demand, and when demand falls, inventories and production levels must fall as well. First, production will be curtailed to prevent further inventory buildup, and then, rather than hold excess material in inventory, companies will drop their prices in order to meet their own cash needs. They may even liquidate inventories at a loss, in order to survive the slump.

It should be obvious, however, that the price reductions cannot be permanent unless the production costs fall. At some point, the liquidating company will be rid of its excess inventory, and it will not resume production unless the price rises to a profitable level again. Eventually, the supply will fall until it equals the lower demand, and at that point the price will rise again, stabilizing at the cost of production plus a reasonable profit.

The Level Three Alpha Strategist is interested in storing value for long periods. The fact that the price of a metal will always be pulled toward the optimum profit level for the producers is his guarantee that if he buys at this level or any lower level, the metal will, over the long pull, be certain to protect the purchasing power of his wealth. No matter how fast inflation races ahead, production costs will follow, and eventually, so will the price of the metal.

Determining Production Costs

While the logic of buying when prices are near or below production cost is sound, the Alpha Strategist will usually find it difficult to determine this cost. First, it is rare that a mine produces only one metal; an ore body may produce several, and although one may be the primary metal in the ore, all the metals are recovered, and each will contribute to the income from mining. Thus, a copper mine may produce silver as a byproduct, or vice-versa, and it is impossible to sort out the true production cost of one or the other.

Second, every mine has its own cost of production. Some bodies of ore have high concentrations of metal and others have low concentrations. It may cost the same to process the ore whether ten pounds or 100 pounds of metal are recovered per ton of ore. Furthermore, mines of equivalent ore grades may have substantially different costs of processing, depending on the equipment they use, and the cost of labor, taxes, etc., in the area in which they are located. Governments of some countries often subsidize the production of certain metals, thus distorting the picture even more.

When actual production costs are not available, the Alpha

Strategist can take several approaches to judging how the current price of a metal relates to the production cost.

First, the price history of the metal is helpful, since the average price is probably close to actual production cost plus a profit. Prices are at times higher than this level, and at times lower, and the long-term trend will tend to match the rate of inflation. Anytime the price of a metal falls near its base trend-line, it can be assumed to be a reasonable purchase. Second, many brokerage firms and industry organizations offer publications that discuss the production costs, and these sources sometimes provide general information that can aid the true saver. Finally, if no reliable information can be found, just monitoring the health of the industry will usually be sufficient. When metal producers are dropping prices, closing mines, and begging governments for assistance, it can be assumed that prices are below the levels where producers can make a profit. These are the times to add to your savings.

Buying & Storing

There are two ways to buy metals: you can buy them from metals brokers, whom you'll find listed in the Yellow Pages of most large cities, or you can buy some of them on the commodities futures exchanges. The small investor may find it difficult to deal with metals brokers, primarily because of the problems of reselling the metals back into the market at the point he wishes to liquidate his holdings. When arranging to purchase any of the metals, it is best to discuss this problem with the broker, and try to secure his agreement to repurchase at some predetermined discount from the spot price. Providing the order is reasonably substantial, and the metal is properly warehoused, he may be willing to do this.

Commodity Exchanges

The commodity exchanges offer a good source for the purchase of certain metals. The U.S. exchanges offer contracts in gold, silver, platinum, copper, and zinc. The London Metal Exchange offers contracts in silver, copper, zinc, lead, tin, nickel, and aluminum.

Most investors have little experience in commodities futures contracts, and regard the futures market as a very high-risk medium. In practice, futures contracts can be approached in one of two ways: the investor can speculate in commodities by buying contracts on high-margin, and trading in and out according to some system (truly a high-risk proposition); or, he can simply use the exchanges as a low-cost source for purchasing the physical commodities, in which case there is no more risk than buying through a metals broker.

A commodity exchange is just a place where a person who wants to buy something and a person who wants to sell it get together through a broker and make an agreement to exchange. The broker's job is to bring the two together, handle the paperwork, and make certain that the agreements are fulfilled. For this, he receives a commission, usually between $50 and $100 from the buyer and the same from the seller for each contract traded.

The exchange designs standard contracts for each commodity which specify the amount and grade of the commodity being traded, the terms under which it will be delivered to the buyer, and the date on which the delivery is to take place. For example, the New York Commodities Exchange (Comex) offers copper in 25,000 pound contracts for delivery on the last trading day of January, March, May, June, July, September, and December of each year. The exchange determines the minimum amount of cash a buyer must deposit in order to arrange for delivery of a contract (minimum margin), as well as the minimum amount a seller must put up in order to guarantee that he can deliver the copper when the delivery date rolls around. This minimum varies but is normally about 5 percent to 10 percent of the contract's total value. When prices become very volatile, or when the exchange wants to control speculation, the minimum may be raised to as much as 50 percent of the contract's value. In the case of copper, if copper is selling at

$1.00 per pound, a contract to purchase 25,000 pounds would be valued at $25,000 and the minimum margin will usually be from $1,500 to $6,000.

Why Commodity Traders Lose

Most buyers and sellers in the futures markets are speculators. That is, the buyers buy contracts for future delivery on the speculation that the value of the commodity will rise before the delivery date rolls around, and thus they can sell their contract for a profit. The sellers sell contracts on the speculation that the price of the commodity will fall before delivery date rolls around, and thus they can profit on the price decline.

Properly viewed, the speculators who buy and sell contracts are nothing more than gamblers who bet against one another. Each normally puts down minimum margin, and buys and sells frequently, betting on short-term moves. When two players wager against each other in a game of chance, one cannot win more than the other loses. When a portion of each bet goes to the dealer, however, the two players can both come out losers. If two players each start with $1,000, and the dealer takes $100 out of each bet, after twenty bets both of them will be broke and the dealer will be $2,000 richer.

This is what happens in the commodity markets for most speculators. Brokers take only about $50 commission per contract from a player, but this represents an average of around 5 percent of the margin put up by the player. An active trader will turn over contracts at least every month, and sometimes weekly or daily. It takes little time—twenty trades or so—and the total margin has been lost to commissions. Commodity brokers usually figure that they will earn 25 to 30 percent of the total value of a client's margin *every year*. If the two opposing players each lose 25 percent of their capital to the broker each year, is it any wonder that the commodities futures game is considered risky?

The irony is that each player, both the buyer and seller, really believes that he can predict the short-term moves in commodity prices. But he cannot. Not only has research proven that short-term movements in stock prices are random, it has also proven that short-term price movements in commodities are random as well. Individuals who make short-term trades in commodities are playing against odds that are equally as bad as the odds on the roulette wheel in Las Vegas. No one should continue trading commodities without first investigating the evidence for randomness in prices described in David Dreman's book *Contrarian Investment Strategy*, as cited in Chapter Six.

In spite of the fact that the futures market is primarily used as a wild gaming pit by speculators, it also has another side. It offers an unusual opportunity to the conservative, prudent Alpha Strategist. Buried among all the traps and dangers is a way that an individual investor can buy commodities at a very low commission, hold them for long periods without taking delivery, or, if he chooses, take delivery, and then have a ready, waiting market for resale on a moment's notice by simply picking up the telephone and making one call.

Buying a contract for future delivery is much the same as putting something on layaway at a department store. You make a deposit and agree to pay the balance when you pick up the merchandise. In exchange for your commitment to buy, the store agrees to a price, holds the merchandise for you, and delivers it at the agreed time.

To buy metals on the futures exchange, you place an order for the number of contracts you want through any registered broker (most stock brokerage firms deal in commodities contracts). On the American commodities exchanges, copper and zinc are the only industrial metals available, and zinc has been traded so little that there is a possibility it may be dropped. Copper, however, offers a good opportunity for the Alpha Strategist. Copper contracts on the Comex are for 25,000 pounds of the metal, plus or minus 2 percent. The physical copper may be in the form of cathodes, wirebar, or ingots, and slight adjustments to the price will be made to compensate for the slightly different values of these forms at the time of delivery.

When placing an order, you will specify the month in which you want the copper delivered, and pay the broker a deposit, normally between 5 and 25 percent of the value of the contract. The copper is stored in Comex-approved warehouses in various locations around the country. When the delivery date rolls around, you pay the broker the balance of the total contract price, plus his commission (usually around $50), and you'll receive a warehouse receipt for the copper which will tell you where it's located, and give you title. If you want to leave it in the warehouse, you can arrange to pay the storage costs, plus a modest amount for insurance, and it can stay there. Storage and insurance costs vary, but you will probably pay in the neighborhood of $2.00 per ton per month. Since each contract is for 12.5 tons, you'll be paying about $300 per year per contract for storage. If the metal is worth $1.00 per pound, your storage and insurance will be costing you just over 1 percent per year.

If you don't move the copper out of the approved warehouse, selling is just a matter of placing a sell order with your broker and handling the paperwork necessary to transfer title.

The advantage of taking delivery is that you can hold the copper for years without worrying about taxes on gains. If copper moves up with inflation, you will not incur a tax liability until you sell.

It is not necessary to take delivery of the metal in order to hold title to it, as your futures contract is your claim. You can buy a contract for a distant delivery month (as far away as twenty-three months), put down your margin, and keep the balance of the purchase price in a money-market fund or in Treasury bills, thus earning interest. If you study the copper futures prices in your metropolitan newspaper or the Wall Street Journal, you will notice that nearby contracts are priced lower than distant contracts. Usually, this difference approximates the interest cost on money for the number of months of the contract; thus, the interest you earn by putting the balance of your contract price in T-bills will offset the contract price differential.

When the delivery date of your contract rolls around, it still isn't necessary to take delivery of the metal in order to maintain your position. Any time before the due date, instruct your broker to sell that contract, and to buy another one for delivery twenty-three months later. You can continue to roll contracts over for years in this manner, always owning the raw commodity, but never taking delivery. One disadvantage to this is that there will be a commission each time you roll over, and each rollover will result in a gain or loss that must be reported on your income tax return.

The value of metals fluctuates hourly when trading is open. If you put down a deposit of $3,000 on a contract valued at $25,000, and the value of the contract subsequently falls to $20,000, your margin deposit will not be sufficient to cover the loss, and since your broker doesn't want to risk his own money, he constantly monitors the value of the contract versus the amount of margin you have on deposit. When the value of the contract falls to the point that you might go into a loss position, he will call and ask you to put up more margin. If you refuse, he will sell your contract in order to protect himself. This does not present a problem to the Alpha Strategist, as he should have the total amount of the contract price either in the bank, T-bills, or some other liquid form at all times, and merely needs to transfer the funds to the broker.

A few caveats are in order regarding dealing in the futures market.

Don't buy options. Option premiums are high, options are for short periods, and the option premium does not apply to the purchase price. Options do not meet the criteria of the Alpha Strategy for true savings of long-term store-of-value assets.

Don't buy nearby contracts. Your broker will do his utmost to induce you to buy contracts with nearby delivery dates. His commission is paid when the contract is closed out, so if you buy distant contracts he won't be paid until then. Furthermore, if you intend to retain your position in a commodity, buying nearby contracts means you must roll your positions over more often. This is profitable for the broker, but unprofitable for you. The broker will give you more reasons for buying nearby contracts than a life insurance salesman will give you for buying cash-value life insurance. Don't listen to either of them.

Don't trade. Your broker will call you regularly, alerting you to every change in the market, and urging you to buy or sell because of this or that news. Ignore him. The Alpha Strategy is a savings plan, not a system for speculation. Trading makes brokers rich and traders poor. Don't trade.

These brief discussions of the futures markets and copper contracts are not meant to give you a complete understanding of these vehicles, nor a detailed program for integrating them into your Alpha Strategy portfolio. There are many nuances to the commodities markets, and a wide range of acceptable commodities can be used to preserve your wealth. Besides the metals, there are a variety of other storable commodities to consider, such as oil, lumber, plywood, and cotton. There are also commodities markets and exchanges in other parts of the world. London offers a much wider range of metals, and although the futures contracts are much shorter, taking delivery and storing your stockpile there may be the best bet. In addition, you have the advantage of having part of your wealth stored outside the United States. As our political problems grow deeper, you may find this to be a very major benefit.

Anyone who wants to understand and use raw commodities as a vehicle for storing wealth can get a thorough introduction and on-going recommendations by subscribing to *The Metals Investor*, a monthly newsletter devoted entirely to the subject of investing in industrial and strategic metals. The publication covers both speculative and saving strategies, discusses sources for purchasing, storing, and reselling (both in the U.S. and abroad), and presents a continuing commentary on production, industrial consumption, government regulations, and investor interest on over twenty metals. For information, write to:

The Metals Investor
711 West 17th St., Suite G-4
Costa Mesa, California 92627

Conclusion

Raw industrial commodities offer the safest, soundest opportunity for preserving wealth that exists in the world today. The saver of these forms of real wealth forgoes the dream of immense speculative profits, but is assured of protection against the risks of inflation, volatile markets, and speculation. Properly purchased and stored, raw industrial commodities are a near-perfect inflation hedge. Perhaps the only one that exists.

At this point you have been exposed to the underlying causes of inflation, depression, and the volatility of investment values, and have been presented with a safe, rational strategy for completely protecting your wealth against all three. Unfortunately, the Alpha Strategy offers little opportunity for huge gains, and in this age of wild speculation, many readers will pass it over in favor of the lure of instant wealth promised by so many of the popular investment schemes.

The wise person, however, is one who puts life's odds in his own favor by correctly assessing the probabilities of gain or loss. The economic events of the coming decade are certain to be the most traumatic of this century. Fortunes will be made and fortunes will be lost, but, without question, there will be far more losers than winners. Better to take your profits while you can and hide them from the ravages to come than to make that last wild bet in hopes of doubling your stake. The odds are against the poor saver and investor who build their futures on the gamble of paper claims, and totally in favor of those who turn instead to real, tangible wealth.

CHAPTER ELEVEN

LEVEL FOUR: TOWARD A THEFT-FREE FUTURE

The most profound and baffling mystery since the beginning of civilization has been the mystery of why societies decay. In every century, in every nation, men have lived in frustration, knowing they were being victimized, yet unable to pinpoint the cause of the violent economic turmoil that relentlessly destroyed their nations.

For centuries men have been baffled by this mystery because they have overlooked the single key that could differentiate between positive and negative human actions. By wrongly guessing that greed and profit were the root of man's troubles, the attack has been leveled at man's greatest benefactor: production. By completely misunderstanding the forms theft can take, as well as the deadly effects it has on human relationships, we have allowed the plunderers to work without detection.

The profit motive is not the culprit. Getting the most we can from the things we own and produce is inherent in our nature. Selfishness is the evolutionary heritage of life itself. The individual, whether laborer or businessman, is not guilty of causing inflation, depression, or monetary turmoil simply by demanding more for his production. The individual, whether laborer or businessman, does not cause scarcity, or want, simply by acting aggressively to win your business from his competitor. Just the opposite: these acts of blatant self-interest and intense competitive wrestling are the very things that generate a flood of innovation and production for the benefit of all.

The culprit is theft—particularly that insidious, nearly undetectable plunder carried out under the cloak of legality. Here businessmen, laborers, and consumers all stand guilty, for by blocking competition through regulation, and stealing through taxation and inflation, the manipulators of government force have topped the economy of every society in history, just as they are bringing down our economy today.

I hope you feel, as you come to the final pages of this book, that you have at last seen through the sham. I also hope that you not only know who the con men really are, but that you now know how to protect your wealth and insure your own financial survival. Even if you do, however, you may still feel unsatisfied, for if you're a thinker, you must now be asking the final, great questions: How can the theft be stopped? How can the cancerous growth of government be checked, and reversed? How can we disarm the State?

Like the Wizard of Oz, the State appears all-powerful, benevolent, unchallengeable, the maker of miracles, the source of wealth, and the protector of the rights of all. Political leaders parade before us with pomp and ceremony, in one era borne about in gilded carriages, in another era carried in shining, bullet-proof limousines. They ponder the deep problems of the world in the secrecy of awesome marble temples, counseling with the wisest of the sorcerers, the highest priests of wisdom and knowledge from the greatest universities. Deified by the masses, they smile before the ovations of the crowds, here and there blessing a few of the fortunate with a word, a memento, an appointment. They talk of greatness, of nation, of honor, of struggle, and sacrifice. They rest their fingers atop the buttons of Armageddon.

Most people feel the world's exalted leaders have access to knowledge and secrets that normal citizens can never share, and that if the problems of mankind can be solved, these leaders will solve them. Unfortunately, those in power have only one secret of consequence that is not shared by all. They know that the authority of the State is a fraud. Any rational person can understand the solutions to the problems of society just as well as the politicians and their advisers. In fact, after reading this book, you know more about how the world really works, and more about the solutions to the problems of society, than any politician or bureaucrat.

The naked truth is that the State, like the Wizard, does not exist. The government is merely a thought, an agreement among men, a figment of imagination. It is an illusion, just as the Wizard's face seen through the smoke and flames by Dorothy, the Cowardly Lion, the Tinman, and the Scarecrow was an illusion. All that exist are single individuals, just like you and me. The majestic voice of government, like the booming voice heard by Dorothy and her friends, is not a voice of supreme power. It is the voice of one other individual being amplified through a tunnel of culture that has indoctrinated us all with a blind belief in the authority of the State. If you pull back the curtain, you will find an individual, just like yourself, desperately talking into the microphone. He knows that he is not all-powerful, that he has no lasting answers, and that he can retain his control only as long as he makes individuals believe he can grant wishes. But he has no magic. If he grants a wish to one, it is only by taking the item granted from someone else.

It is the people in line who give power to the voice of government. Millions of individuals stand in line, each waiting his turn to request a benefit, to secure the use of force against a competitor, and to get his fair share of the plunder. If you look carefully, you will see many of the people you know standing there, eager to have a wish granted. There is the manufacturer seeking a tariff, the union member seeking minimum wage laws, the troubled employer seeking government subsidy, the unemployed worker seeking unemployment benefits, the government employee waiting for his pension. Perhaps you have stood there yourself. If you would search for the root of all social ills, don't bother with the man at the microphone; look past him to all the outstretched hands. The culprits? In the immortal words of Walt Kelly's Pogo, "We have met the enemy, and he is us."

There is only one source of wealth: production. The more you produce, the more you will have. If the citizens of a nation want a higher standard of living, those same citizens must produce more. The laws of economics merely describe human motivation and human behavior. These laws tell us that a higher standard of living cannot result from tearing the fruits of one man's labor away from him and bestowing them on another. Yet the majority of mankind remains convinced that this is how progress comes about. Indeed, the use of government as a sword of theft has been perfected in our society today. You have the dubious honor of being a victim of the greatest sting in the history of mankind.

What, then, is the answer? Is it to devote our lives to ridding politics of those individuals who plunder us? Should we use the political process to establish honest government once and for all? Should we campaign, vote, lobby, protest, and demonstrate?

It is an attractive thought, but how does that course differ from what has always been tried?

Political action has a clear track throughout history. It consists of concerted attempts by righteous and concerned citizens to throw the "bad guys" out. The belief that society could be perfected by eliminating the bad guys began long before Brutus and his fellow senators drove their knives into Caesar. It has been the predominant belief throughout the ages, and it is the overwhelming attitude of almost everyone in the world today. Only, no matter how forcefully the bad guys are thrown out of office, they always seem to be replaced by another group who turn out to be equally bad, if not worse. The political experience in the United States certainly confirms this pattern. We have had endless changes of faces in local, state, and federal offices for two hundred years in this country—yet freedom deteriorates year after year. Doesn't it seem that at some point the political process itself might be questioned?

Throwing the bad guys out is not the answer, because the bad guys are not in office to begin with. Politicians and bureaucrats are not your problem. They never have been and they never will be. Your life is being disrupted, and your property stolen, not by the politicians and bureaucrats, *but by the people who hire them*. It is not the man at the microphone, but the people in line. This is why the sting has been so incredibly successful for such a vast span of time: attention has always been focused on the political process, and the attack has always been aimed in that direction.

Pretend for a moment that you have cultivated a cabbage patch on your island, and Maynard has some goats. Every night Maynard opens your gate and lets his goats into your yard, and each night they feast on your cabbages. You decide to approach the problem by appealing to reason. You put together your arguments about how this is ruining your garden, stifling your incentive to grow cabbages, and will hurt the whole neighborhood in the end. You then walk out of your house, march down to your garden, and have a heart-to-heart talk with his goats.

A ridiculous approach, you say? Of course. While the goats are the ones who eat your cabbages, Maynard is the one who milks the goats. In the end, he is the beneficiary of their theft—he is the culprit who must be dealt with. Even if you find a way to communicate with the goats, it will not help. No matter how many goats you succeed in winning over to your point of view, the moment a goat sees the light and agrees to stop eating your cabbages, Maynard will stop getting milk. Immediately, Maynard will rid himself of that goat and replace it with another one that will eat your cabbages again. So it is with politicians. Even if you convince one to stop plundering you, he will be quickly replaced.

It would appear, then, that the answer must be in the education of the masses to their own long-term self-interest. As I mentioned earlier, if individuals could be convinced that the short-term benefits gained from stealing through inflation, taxation, and regulation were far short of the long-run damage they suffer from these evils, then perhaps they would agree to stop stealing. Certainly, there are many ethical, moral individuals who refuse to use government as a means of plundering their fellow citizens, and the world is better because of them. But the idea of building a moral oasis in the desert of theft is, unfortunately, a utopian concept in itself. The average person is not intelligent enough to value the benefits that an inflation-free, stable, prosperous economy might bring him many years in the future, over the immediate gain he might get by defeating his competitor with government force today. Trying to convince the masses to abandon government favors by appealing to their longer-run self-interest is as futile as trying to convince a five-year-old child not to eat sweets because of the danger of diabetes in old age. Humans are essentially shortsighted and selfish (which is not a condemnation, but a fact of evolution). Each will tend to take the shortest path to achieve his goals, and any solution to our social problems must be consistent with this inherent human quality. We cannot change the nature of man; the solution must come from recognizing that nature, and using it to assist the change.

Man will steal if he perceives it to be the best way to get what he wants. He is primarily interested in satisfying his immediate needs, not in providing for some distant future. He cannot be educated to altruism. In a political democracy that gives a voter the power to confiscate the wealth of his neighbors, human nature guarantees that he will do so. In my estimation, neither politics nor moral preaching offers a rational, workable solution, and it would seem that the historical evidence corroborates this. If the political process is not the answer, and educating the masses is impossible, is there any solution? If there is, where does it lie?

Right under our noses. The best solution is the simplest solution, and the simplest solution is the easiest to overlook. Anyone who has studied the evolution of species has observed the solution at work in every form of life. The solution can be understood by observing the way in which all life forms cope with their hostile environments. The theft of our property by others is an attack that is essentially identical to the destruction that any species feels from any hostile force in nature.

When a species is threatened by forces in its environment, it does not survive by calling a referendum of all the members of the species and attempting to organize all the individuals to fight the invader. Instead, each individual is faced with defending himself as best he can. The individuals that develop a successful technique live to bear offspring, and those that do not, die out. Eventually, the survivors all have defenses that make the invader unable to successfully attack, and either the invader dies out, or he moves on to attack other, more vulnerable prey.

Examples abound in nature. Some butterflies have developed a bitter taste, to discourage birds from eating them. In their pupal stages some moths resemble twigs, so they cannot be seen. The bee grows a poison stinger to fend off its enemies. The important thing to note is that successfully repelling a threat to the survival of the species consists of each individual doing his best to defend himself. The defenses of taste, camouflage, and poison were not a conscious decision of the species, but merely the automatic result of the fact that nature favors those individuals that have developed special defenses, and they live to propagate their species. The instinct for self-preservation is synonymous with selfishness, and is a built-in mechanism in every individual.

Fortunately, man has developed language, and solutions to social problems do not necessarily have to take thousands of generations to spread through the culture.

The way to build a free society and to abolish all of the economic and social destruction that has been man's lot all these many centuries is a simple three-step process. First, correctly identify the direction from which the individual is being attacked. Second, make the individual aware of the nature and methods of his enemy. And third, leave it up to the individual to devise methods for self-defense. Just as a person will try to increase his wealth and comfort by the most effective method (plundering, if that is effective, and producing, if hard work is effective), once he owns something, he will vigorously defend it. The answer to change is not an attack on government, *but the development of individual techniques for the defense of personal property.*

Just as there is no way to know whether an insect will eventually thwart its predator adversaries by making itself bitter-tasting, by disguising itself as a twig, or by developing a poison sting, there is no way for us to anticipate exactly what novel defense mechanisms will come from the efforts of millions of individuals working in their own self-interest. The defenses that will eventually thwart the ability of others to use government force as a method of plundering you are yet to be designed, but their ultimate invention is guaranteed by the natural forces of evolution. But before individuals can begin to innovate effective defenses against being plundered, they must understand how they are being attacked, and by whom.

In the past, man has incorrectly identified the direction from which he has been attacked. Almost everyone has assumed that the politicians and bureaucrats are the enemy. Thus a continued attack has been mounted against government. The cry is always, "let's throw out the bad guys." It can't be done. The individuals in government are merely the hired agents of the real culprits. Government has been a near-perfect decoy, drawing all the attention away from the real thieves; consequently, all defensive efforts have been wasted in a futile political battle to throw out the bad guys. It is clearly a case where the predators, those who feed on the wealth of others through government, have developed such perfect camouflage that their victims have been helpless to develop an effective defense.

The answer to the dilemma that has plagued mankind throughout history is not a quick panacea. It is a slow but certain process that relies on the selfish instinct of each individual. It takes into consideration the fact that individuals are more interested in immediate benefits than in long-term pleasures. Each of us is concerned when someone steals from us, and we will respond immediately to protect our property, provided we understand how we are being plundered. That is the key to change. Individuals must be shown how they are being plundered, and when enough of them are aware, they will individually begin to develop defense mechanisms to cope with the attackers. Eventually, successful mechanisms will be adopted by others, and those that are not successful will be abandoned. The spread of right ideas is inexorable. It is evolution itself.

What are the steps that you might take to begin bringing about lasting change? I have only a few tentative suggestions, which seem to me to be correct, but which may or may not be the most effective answers. The ingenuity of hundreds and thousands of others applied to this problem will result in discovery of many other answers, and some will certainly be more effective than these preliminary steps.

Step One is to defend your own wealth. Saving real wealth protects your wealth against the predators, and is a first and important step in making it unprofitable for them to continue their actions. The Alpha Strategy has positive steps that every individual can take immediately.

Step Two is to make the plunderers aware that you have caught on to their game. Your time and energy are limited, so don't waste them on any efforts to fight the government, or government policies. Remember, government is a decoy. Direct all your attention to exposing the real thieves. This can be done in many ways. For example, when you hear about a company requesting a subsidy from the government, don't write to your politician. Write, instead, to the president of that company, and tell him just exactly what you think about his action. When you hear about a business lobbying for a tariff, or a regulation to inhibit competition, bypass your politician. Contact that company directly and let its owners know how you feel. When you find a union pleading for laws to prevent other laborers from competing for jobs, let your voice be heard—not by your congressman, but by the members of that union. Remember that many of these individuals do not even understand that their use of government is actually theft. Explain your position clearly, and ask them to stop.

Everyone knows how difficult it is to get the attention of politicians. Businessmen, however, have a much more direct and immediate stake in what you have to say. When you find one trying to destroy his competitor with government force, tell him that you know exactly what he is doing, and that you will boycott his products and publicize his theft until he stops. It is that simple. When customers begin boycotting products, businessmen must pay attention.

Rather than send a lobbying team to pressure the politicians into changing laws in your favor, instead devote energy to analyzing the lobbying efforts of others. Find out who is pressuring the politicians for special privilege, and then go directly to those individuals. Pull away the cloak of government that they are hiding behind, and expose them for everyone to see. If enough people start pointing the finger of responsibility in the right direction, at the people who are really the thieves and swindlers, future history books will mark that point as the beginning of change.

Step Three is to alert your friends and neighbors to the nature of the sting, and to all of the confidence games being promoted in this economic carnival. Alert them to the direction from which the attack is coming, so that they can begin to defend their wealth, and work with you to build the barricades in the right place. If you believe this book has been effective in arguing the case for a free market and exposing the sting, recommend it to them. Or write one yourself.

The next decade promises to be the most turbulent decade in this century. The plunder is mounting. The die is cast. The economic storms are unavoidable, and the outcome for most individuals will be the destruction of their wealth.

There is only one alternative to a world of inflation, recession, social conflict, and war: it is a theft-free society. The concept is not utopian. It is consistent with all the laws of economics laid down in Chapter One, and it is in perfect harmony with the principles of evolution. It can be realized, and eventually it will be realized. Whether this theft-free society is achieved in your lifetime or mine depends on how well we each defend our wealth. So go to work, and good luck.

APPENDIX

APPENDIX

SHELF LIVES OF LEVEL FOUR CONSUMABLES

The following items are listed as possible additions to your Alpha Strategy personal stockpile. You will, no doubt, find that many of them are not items you normally consume, and likewise, many items you use regularly will be missing from this list.

Information on shelf lives should be considered only an estimate, as actual shelf lives will depend on a wide range of variables including such things as specific processes used by manufacturers, how the product has been handled, and conditions of temperature, light, and humidity under which it has been and will be stored. Before stockpiling any item, you should verify storage life with the manufacturer.

ITEM	ESTIMATED SHELF LIFE	ITEM	ESTIMATED SHELF LIFE

FOOD

ITEM	ESTIMATED SHELF LIFE	ITEM	ESTIMATED SHELF LIFE
Beans (dried)		Pepper	*Indefinite*
Lima	*10 years*	Rice	*10 years*
Pinto	*10 years*	Salt	*Indefinite*
Red	*10 years*	Soda	*Indefinite*
Cocoa	*15 months*	Soy sauce	*Indefinite*
Corn starch	*5-10 years*	Sugar	
Gelatin	*3 years*	White	*Indefinite*
Honey	*Indefinite*	Brown	*Indefinite*
Jams	*Indefinite*	Powdered	*Indefinite*
Jellies	*Indefinite*	Syrup	*Indefinite*
Liquor		Tea	*Indefinite*
Scotch	*Indefinite*	Vinegar	*5 years*
Bourbon	*Indefinite*	Wheat	*Indefinite*
Vodka	*Indefinite*	Wine	*Varies*
Gin	*Indefinite*	Vitamin A	*2 years*
Macaroni	*5 years*	Vitamin B	*3-5 years*
Molasses	*Indefinite*	Vitamin C	*5 years*
Noodles	*5 years*	Vitamin E	*2 years*
Peas/dried	*10 years*	Multiple vitamins	*3 years*

HEALTH AND BEAUTY PRODUCTS

ITEM	SHELF LIFE	ITEM	SHELF LIFE
Adhesive tape	*Indefinite*	Chap stick	*1 year*
After shave	*Indefinite*	Chest rubs	*Indefinite*
Alcohol	*Indefinite*	Curlers	*Indefinite*
Antacid	*Indefinite*	Combs	*Indefinite*
Antiseptics	*Indefinite*	Cotton	*Indefinite*
BandAids	*5 years*	Cotton balls	*Indefinite*
Baby powder	*Indefinite*	Cough syrup	*Indefinite*
Bath oil	*Indefinite*	Dental floss	*Indefinite*
Bubble bath	*2 years*	Denture cleanser	*Indefinite*
Bobby pins	*Indefinite*	Denture adhesives	*Indefinite*
Breath fresheners	*3 years*	Deodorants	*Indefinite*

| ITEM | ESTIMATED SHELF LIFE | ITEM | ESTIMATED SHELF LIFE |

HEALTH AND BEAUTY PRODUCTS (continued)

Emery boards.........*Indefinite*
Epsom salts...........*Indefinite*
Face creams............*2 years*
Hair nets.............*Indefinite*
Hair spray ....*1 year*
Hair conditioner........*Indefinite*
Hair shampoo..........*Indefinite*
Hairwave sets..........*Indefinite*
Headache remedies .....*Indefinite*
Hand lotion.............*2 years*
Laxatives................*1 year*
Mouthwash..............*3 years*
Nail files ....*Indefinite*
Nail polish remover.....*Indefinite*

Peroxide..............*Indefinite*
Razor blades...........*Indefinite*
Razors ....*Indefinite*
Sanitary napkins..........*2 years*
Soap
    Hand ....*Indefinite*
    Shaving ....*Indefinite*
Tampons ....*2 years*
Tanning lotions...........*2 years*
Throat lozenges ....*Indefinite*
Toothbrushes ....*Indefinite*
Toothpaste ....*Indefinite*
Vaseline..............*Indefinite*

CLEANING SUPPLIES

Ammonia.............*Indefinite*
Bleach ....*Indefinite*
Brooms..............*Indefinite*
Brushes ....*Indefinite*
Cleansers.............*Indefinite*
Cleaning fluids ....*Indefinite*
Copper cleaners........*Indefinite*
Dish soap...............*2 years*
Dishwasher soap ....*2 years*
Disinfectants..........*Indefinite*
Drain openers..........*Indefinite*
Fabric softeners ....*Indefinite*
Floor wax ....*Indefinite*
Furniture polish ....*Indefinite*

Garbage cans ....*Indefinite*
Glass cleaners ....*Indefinite*
Insecticides ....*Indefinite*
Laundry additives.........*2 years*
Laundry detergent ....*2 years*
Rug cleaners ....*Indefinite*
Scouring pads..........*Indefinite*
Scrub brushes..........*Indefinite*
Silver polish ....*Indefinite*
Sponges ....*Indefinite*
Starch................*Indefinite*
Toilet bowl cleaners ....*Indefinite*
Trash bags.............*Indefinite*
Trash compactor bags...*Indefinite*

ITEM	ESTIMATED SHELF LIFE	ITEM	ESTIMATED SHELF LIFE

PAPER & PLASTIC PRODUCTS

Aluminum foil. . . . . *Indefinite*		Paper plates. . . . . *5-10 years*	
Disposable diapers. . . . . . . *2 years*		Paper towels . . . . *5 years*	
Drop cloths . . . . *Indefinite*		Plastic wrap . . . . *Indefinite*	
Envelopes . . . . *5 years*		Sandwich bags . . . . *Indefinite*	
Facial tissues . . . . *5 years*		Toilet paper. . . . . *5 years*	
Gift wrap. . . . . *5 years*		Trash bags. . . . . *Indefinite*	
Notebook paper . . . . *5 years*		Vacuum bags. . . . . *5 years*	
Paper cups. . . . . *5-10 years*		Wax paper. . . . . *Indefinite*	

HOME & YARD MAINTENANCE

Brushes . . . . *Indefinite*		Paint. . . . . *Indefinite*	
Caulking. . . . . *18-24 months*		Plant vitamins. . . . . *Indefinite*	
Drill bits . . . . *Indefinite*		Plastic sheeting. . . . . *Indefinite*	
Electrical tape. . . . . *Indefinite*		Pliers . . . . *Indefinite*	
Extension cords . . . . *Indefinite*		Rakes . . . . *Indefinite*	
Faucet repair kits. . . . . . . *Indefinite*		Sandpaper . . . . *Indefinite*	
Fertilizer . . . . *Indefinite*		Saw blades . . . . *Indefinite*	
Flower pots. . . . . *Indefinite*		Screening. . . . . *Indefinite*	
Furnace filters . . . . *Indefinite*		Screws . . . . *Indefinite*	
Glue . . . . *2 years*		Screwdrivers . . . . *Indefinite*	
Hacksaw blades . . . . *Indefinite*		Seeds	
Hammers. . . . . *Indefinite*		Flower . . . . *1-7 years*	
Hand trowels . . . . *Indefinite*		Grass . . . . *2-3 years*	
Hedge clippers . . . . *Indefinite*		Vegetable. . . . . *3-5 years*	
Hoes. . . . . *Indefinite*		Shovels. . . . . *Indefinite*	
Hoses . . . . *Indefinite*		Sponges . . . . *Indefinite*	
Insecticides . . . . *Indefinite*		Sprinkler parts . . . . *Indefinite*	
Lawnmower parts. . . . . . . *Indefinite*		Toggle bolts. . . . . *Indefinite*	
Light bulbs . . . . *Indefinite*		Wall anchors. . . . . *Indefinite*	
Nails. . . . . *Indefinite*		Water softener salt . . . . . *Indefinite*	
Paint brushes . . . . *Indefinite*		Wire . . . . *Indefinite*	
Paint rollers. . . . . *Indefinite*		Work gloves . . . . *Indefinite*	

ITEM	ESTIMATED SHELF LIFE	ITEM	ESTIMATED SHELF LIFE

AUTO MAINTENANCE

ITEM	ESTIMATED SHELF LIFE	ITEM	ESTIMATED SHELF LIFE
Air filters	*Indefinite*	Motor oil	*Indefinite*
Anti-freeze	*Indefinite*	Oil additives	*Indefinite*
Batteries	*Indefinite*	Polish	*Indefinite*
Brake fluid	*Indefinite*	Radiator hoses	*Indefinite*
Carburetor cleaner	*Indefinite*	Spark plugs	*Indefinite*
Fan belts	*Indefinite*	Tires	*Indefinite*
Gasoline	*1 year*	Transmission fluid	*Indefinite*
Ignition sets	*Indefinite*	Wax	*Indefinite*

CLOTHING—MEN'S

ITEM	ESTIMATED SHELF LIFE	ITEM	ESTIMATED SHELF LIFE
Bathrobes	*Indefinite*	Shorts	*Indefinite*
Belts	*Indefinite*	Slippers	*Indefinite*
Dress shirts	*Indefinite*	Snow hats	*Indefinite*
Gloves	*Indefinite*	Socks	*Indefinite*
Handkerchiefs	*Indefinite*	Sweat shirts	*Indefinite*
Jeans	*Indefinite*	Sweat pants	*Indefinite*
Long underwear	*Indefinite*	Sweaters	*Indefinite*
Mittens	*Indefinite*	T-Shirts	*Indefinite*
Overcoats	*Indefinite*	Undershirts	*Indefinite*
Pajamas	*Indefinite*	Work shirts	*Indefinite*
Rain gear	*Indefinite*	Work pants	*Indefinite*

CLOTHING—WOMEN'S

ITEM	ESTIMATED SHELF LIFE	ITEM	ESTIMATED SHELF LIFE
Bathrobes	*Indefinite*	Slippers	*Indefinite*
Bras	*Indefinite*	Socks	*Indefinite*
Gloves	*Indefinite*	Stockings	*Indefinite*
Jeans	*Indefinite*	Sweaters	*Indefinite*
Long underwear	*Indefinite*	Sweat pants	*Indefinite*
Nightgowns	*Indefinite*	Sweat shirts	*Indefinite*
Panties	*Indefinite*	Work shirts	*Indefinite*
Pantyhose	*Indefinite*	Work pants	*Indefinite*
Rain gear	*Indefinite*		

ITEM	ESTIMATED SHELF LIFE	ITEM	ESTIMATED SHELF LIFE

MISCELLANEOUS

Softgoods

Bedspreads .... *Indefinite*
Blankets .... *Indefinite*
Curtains .... *Indefinite*
Dish cloths .... *Indefinite*
Dish towels .... *Indefinite*
Mattress covers .... *Indefinite*
Napkins .... *Indefinite*
Pillows .... *Indefinite*
Pillow cases .... *Indefinite*
Sheets................ *Indefinite*
Tablecloths .... *Indefinite*
Towels .... *Indefinite*
Washcloths .... *Indefinite*

Recreation

Tennis shoes .... *Indefinite*

Golf shoes .... *Indefinite*
Jogging suits .... *Indefinite*

Miscellaneous

Batteries................. *1 year*
Pens .... *1 year*
Flashlights............. *Indefinite*
Needles .... *Indefinite*
Notebooks .... *Indefinite*
Pencils .... *Indefinite*
Pins................... *Indefinite*
Rope.................. *Indefinite*
Scissors .... *Indefinite*
Scotch tape .... *1 year*
Staples .... *Indefinite*
Thread .... *Indefinite*

SELECTED BIBLIOGRAPHY

SELECTED
BIBLIOGRAPHY

The following books are suggested reading for those who would like to explore further the subjects discussed in the text.

On Basic Economics

Hazlitt, Henry. *Economics In One Lesson*. New York: MacFadden-Bartell Corp., 1969. An excellent, short, delightfully readable explanation of basic economics.

Pugsley, John A. *Common Sense Economics*. Costa Mesa, California: Common Sense Press, 2nd Ed., 1976. A view of money, and a guide to personal financial planning for the upper-middle class professional and executive.

Rothbard, Murray N. *Man, Economy, and State*. Los Angeles: Nash Publishing, 1970. An extensive (900+ pages) study of rational economic principles. Written for the intelligent layman, it provides a comprehensive view of the entire subject.

von Mises, Ludwig. *Human Action*. Chicago: Henry Regnery Company, 1949. This is the "bible" for devotees of the Austrian school. Over 900 pages of sometimes difficult, but always profound, ideas.

Weaver, Henry Grady. *The Mainspring of Human Progress*. Irvington-on-Hudson, New York: Foundation for Economic Education, Inc., 1953. A well-written and absorbing account of the origins of human wealth and the nature of freedom. Very worthwhile reading.

232

The History of Inflation

Bresciani-Turroni, Costantino. *The Economics of Inflation.* London: Augustus M. Kelley, 1968. A detailed and occasionally technical account of the great German inflation after World War I.

Graham, Frank D. *Exchange, Prices, and Production in Hyper-Inflation: Germany, 1920–1923.* New York: Russell & Russell, 1967. Another interesting account of the German inflation.

White, Andrew Dickson. *Fiat Money Inflation in France.* Caldwell, Idaho: The Caxton Printers, Ltd., 1972. An absorbing narrative of the events that accompanied the great French inflation during the period of the French Revolution. This is a small but brilliant work by the founder of Cornell University. Absolutely must reading.

On Government Intervention in the Economy

Armentano, D.T. *The Myths of Anti-Trust.* New Rochelle, New York: Arlington House, 1972. An excellent, in-depth discussion of the fallacies of anti-trust laws. Well documented.

Bastiat, Frederic. *Economic Sophisms.* Irvington-on-Hudson, New York: Foundation for Economic Education, Inc., 1964. Bastiat is a master of clarifying economic concepts and destroying the perverse arguments of statist writers. His books should be on every bookshelf.

Bastiat, Frederic. *The Law.* Irvington-on-Hudson, New York: Foundation for Economic Education, Inc., 1968. This tiny book is the best treatise on the use of law as a tool of plunder that exists anywhere. Must reading.

Block, Walter. *Defending the Undefendable.* New York: Fleet Press Corporation, 1976. A delightful, witty, and often shocking argument for allowing individuals total freedom to pursue their own lives, no matter what socially contemptible occupations they might choose. It will expand your mind.

Curtiss, W.M. *The Tariff Idea.* Irvington-on-Hudson, New York: Foundation for Economic Education, Inc., 1953. A thin little book that demolishes the concept of tariffs with brilliant style.

Rand, Ayn. *Atlas Shrugged.* New York: Random House, 1957. A lengthy but absorbing classic. No doubt, the most important novel of our times.

Weidenbaum, Murray L. *The Future of Business Regulation.* New York: AMACOM, 1979. A detailed account of the fallacies behind modern business regulation.

On Investments

Browne, Harry. *New Profits from the Monetary Crisis.* New York: William Morrow and Company, Inc., 1978. Browne is an excellent writer, and a top investment advisor. He led the way in predicting the devaluation of the dollar, and the subsequent price booms in gold, silver, and Swiss francs.

Casey, Douglas R. *Crisis Investing.* Los Angeles: Stratford Press, 1980. A runaway best-selling book by a provocative, bright investment expert. Should be read by anyone interested in stocks, real estate, or precious metals.

Cardiff, Gray Emerson; English, John Wesley. *The Coming Real Estate Crash.* New Rochelle, New York: Arlington House, 1979. Predicts the collapse of real estate prices, with interesting discussions of past crashes.

Dreman, David. *Contrarian Investment Strategy.* New York: Random House, 1979. While this book is ostensibly about the stock market, it should be read by every investor, regardless of which types of assets he prefers. It offers absolutely compelling evidence for the madness of technical analysis, the flaws in fundamental analysis, and the importance of contrary thinking. It should permanently influence your investment philosophy and performance.

Mackay, Charles, LL.D. *Extraordinary Popular Delusions and the Madness of Crowds.* London: Richard Bentley, 1841. One of the world's classic studies of investment insanity. This should be one of the first books any investor reads.

North, Gary. *How You Can Profit from the Coming Price Controls.* Durham, North Carolina: American Bureau of Economic Research, 1978. A thoughtful and incisive study of the effects of price controls and how you can profit from them.

Ruff, Howard J. *How to Prosper During the Coming Bad Years.* New York: Times Books, 1979. A runaway best seller that offers a broad range of advice on investing during times of economic turmoil.

Skousen, Mark. *Playing the Price Controls Game.* New Rochelle, New York: Arlington House, 1977. An excellent study of ways to profit from the coming price controls.

Smith, Jerome. *The Coming Currency Collapse.* New York: Books in Focus, 1980. A thorough analysis of the causes of currency debasement. The book presents a timetable for a slide into hyperinflation, along with an investment program to defend your wealth. The book offers a sound analysis of the nature of money, as well as interesting histories of past inflations.

On Evolution and Human Behavior

Dawkins, Richard. *The Selfish Gene.* New York: Oxford University Press, 1976. Delightful and easy reading. An absorbing study of the ways genes affect our behavior. Since economic behavior is rooted in evolution, the thoughtful reader should gain significant insights into our economic and social problems.

Wilson, Edward O. *On Human Nature.* Cambridge, Massachusetts: Harvard University Press, 1978. The newest release of the dean of the new science of sociobiology. Absolutely essential reading for everyone who wants to understand the evolutionary foundations of human behavior.

Wilson, Edward O. *Sociobiology.* Cambridge, Massachusetts: Harvard University Press, 1975. A massive textbook that exhaustively covers the studies done on insects, birds, and mammals that relate to genetic-based behavior patterns. Although sometimes technical, the book provides fascinating new insights into our own social behavior that must eventually lead to progress in solving the problems of plunder.